Kentucky Hauntings

Kentucky Hauntings

*Homespun Ghost Stories
and Unexplained History*

ROBERTA SIMPSON BROWN AND LONNIE E. BROWN

UNIVERSITY PRESS OF KENTUCKY

Scholarly publisher for the Commonwealth,
serving Bellarmine University, Berea College, Centre
College of Kentucky, Eastern Kentucky University,
The Filson Historical Society, Georgetown College,
Kentucky Historical Society, Kentucky State University,
Morehead State University, Murray State University,
Northern Kentucky University, Transylvania University,
University of Kentucky, University of Louisville,
and Western Kentucky University.

Editorial and Sales Offices: The University Press of Kentucky
663 South Limestone Street, Lexington, Kentucky 40508-4008
www.kentuckypress.com

Library of Congress Cataloging-in-Publication Data

Brown, Roberta Simpson, 1939–
  Kentucky hauntings : homespun ghost stories and unexplained history /
Roberta Simpson Brown and Lonnie E. Brown.
     pages   cm
  ISBN 978-0-8131-4320-0 (hardcover : alk. paper)—
  ISBN 978-0-8131-4382-8 (epub) — ISBN 978-0-8131-4383-5 (pdf)
  1. Haunted places—Kentucky. 2. Ghosts—Kentucky. I. Brown, Lonnie E.
II. Title.
  BF1472.U6B7756 2013
  133.109769—dc23
                          2013018934

This book is printed on acid-free paper meeting
the requirements of the American National Standard
for Permanence in Paper for Printed Library Materials.

Manufactured in the United States of America.

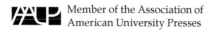 Member of the Association of
American University Presses

To our families and friends,
here and on the other side,
who gave us a love of stories.

And to the late John C. Ferguson,
a great friend, storyteller, and writer.
We thank his wonderful family
for sharing him with us.

Contents

Introduction

Are you ready for some smiles and shivers? The stories in this book will bring you both. In the tradition of Kentucky storytelling, we have included stories that are fun for all ages. We are fortunate to have grown up in a culture that still has storytellers who know the importance of passing stories from one generation to the next. Read these stories, but take them from the page to your imagination. Put them into your own words, and pass them on. In this way you can help these stories from history, headlines, and homefolks live forever.

We are often asked why we enjoy ghost stories and paranormal stories so much. Our answer is simply that they are exciting and fun! The love we had for them as children has carried over into our adult lives.

But scary stories serve more serious purposes than simply being entertaining. They can help us deal with fear. Fear is a universal feeling. Even though we don't all share the same fears, we do share the feeling. Scary stories help us identify our fears and confront them. Only when we do this are we able to control whatever is frightening us. Sharing stories helps us explore ways to deal with our fears. Learning how someone else handles fear can give us insight on how to explore our options and deal with the scary things in our lives. It is also comforting to know that others experience unexplained things as we do, and that helps us affirm our sanity.

We are amazed at the number of people, young and old, who tell us that they have experienced some paranormal experience. Some are confused and do not know what to do. They are afraid to tell anyone else because they are afraid that they will be subjected to ridicule. When they hear or read about an experience similar to their own, they are more inclined to open up and tell about their own experiences. Sometimes, individuals approach us and say that they have a story they want us to use in a book, but more often they just want to relate whatever has been bothering them that they can't explain. They aren't interested in being published. They are only looking for answers.

Storytelling brings us together as a culture. We are close to our families and our neighbors when we sit together, tell stories, and then discuss our feelings about them. Kentucky history is rich in stories passed down from generation to generation. Our heritage lives on through these tales. Our particular area passed on ghost tales. We passed on scary tales because that is what we heard.

People enjoy a good scare, but they don't like the bad kind. A bad scare is, for example, hearing someone breaking into your house or finding yourself in danger, but helpless. A scary story allows you to experience the thrill of being scared while being able to do something about it. You can always stop reading and take a break from the story, or you can cover your ears and avoid listening. In other words, you can take a "fear break" and gather your courage if our stories are too scary.

The stories we tell in these pages were told to us orally, but some accounts have been published in newspapers or posted on the Internet. Although we include notes with each story on any additional sources we used, we have not copied these sources. Rather, we have simply read all we could find about the tales we share here to confirm and provide supporting details for the stories here. We want you, our readers, to feel what the characters feel in the story. Our goal is not only to present facts, but also to write a book you will enjoy reading. So start reading the stories, and bring on the smiles and the shivers.

Stories from History

In our first years of school, we thought history was boring. The teachers we had made us memorize dates and events, but we were not told much about the real people from the past and what they did. Then, when we were in high school, we had a teacher named Mr. Tarter who told us stories that made history come alive. He was able to pull us into those stories and make us feel we were there in a time gone by. It was fascinating to study history from then on.

Another remarkable teacher named Leland Voils, in health class, also told stories, and he made health issues throughout history come alive too. He spoke of characters and events with such vivid detail that we were transported to whatever time period we were studying and we felt what those people must have felt. He was one of the best storytellers we ever met.

Stories give us glimpses into history that we could never see in timelines and strictly factual accounts. Stories paint a mental picture of daily happenings and introduce us to characters that become real in our hearts and minds.

A Chivaree Gone Bad

Roberta's grandmother, Lou Ann Simpson, told about many customs that we did not read about in history books. This is one of her stories.

The chivaree was an odd, but popular, social custom that thrived in Appalachia until the end of World II. It took place in the early evening after a wedding. It was meant originally to scare off evil spirits and to provide an occasion to have some fun with the newlyweds—a kind of old-time version of the modern wedding reception.

In those days, the bride and groom usually had a home of their own to go to after the wedding. Often relatives of the couple helped build the house on land provided by the parents. Money was scarce, so there were practically no honeymoon trips. After the wedding ceremony at the church, the newly married couple would usually stay for a while and mingle with family and friends, who provided food and drinks for the occasion. Then the newlyweds would go to their new house to start their life together.

The chivaree was supposed to be a secret event, but most newlyweds expected it and accepted it as good fun. As dusk approached, relatives and neighbors would gather all the noisemakers they could find—everything from musical instruments to buckets and pots and pans to beat on—and would meet at some common location, like the church. Then they would proceed to the couple's house when it was just about dark.

First, they would march around the house, singing and making as much racket as they could. This usually brought the couple to *the door, but if it didn't, they would stop at the front door and knock. When the couple opened the door, three or four men would grab the groom, seat him astride a split rail from an old rail fence, and carry him off into the woods. Not too far from the house, they would tie him loosely to a tree or a fence post and leave him for a while to see if he could get loose and find his way home by himself. If it took him too long, some of the men would go back and get him.*

While this was going on, the bride would invite all the visitors inside and offer them cookies or cake, with maybe some coffee or lemonade. Sometimes the guests would bring along additional refreshments, and the chivaree would turn into a party. Usually there would be music and dancing until bedtime. By the time the groom rejoined the group, he had usually calmed down if he had been angry, and everybody had a good time, including him.

After we heard this story, we were glad this custom was no longer observed when we got married!

Deep in the Kentucky hills on the first of June many years ago, young Nellie Crenshaw and her longtime love, Jeff Barnes, exchanged vows in the little community church they had attended all their lives. Everybody knew the young couple and showed up to witness their marriage ceremony and to wish them good luck.

It was an especially beautiful wedding. The bride and groom had been childhood sweethearts, and this June day was the fulfillment of their dreams. They had heard whispers of a chivaree, but they went on their way home as if they suspected nothing more. The afternoon passed slowly and the sun set low. They ate an early supper, and Nellie made some cookies and a pot of coffee in anticipation of the visitors they expected to come. Jeff kept looking out the window, not eager for his upcoming role in the night's festivities. Determined to be a good sport, he just wanted to get it over with.

The setting sun was a prearranged signal for the relatives and neighbors to meet in the churchyard. As soon as everybody arrived with their noisemakers, the whole group headed to the young couple's house. Nellie and Jeff listened to the ruckus outside and then opened the door and faced their visitors. The group stopped the noise and began to serenade the young couple with "Let Me Call You Sweetheart." All was calm until the song ended.

As the singers were nearing the end of the song, two men quietly edged their way close to the door. When the last note was sung, they suddenly grabbed the groom, dragged him out into the yard, and seated him on the split rail from the fence. Jeff offered the expected resistance, but went along with the prank. Off they went with him across the field to the woods behind the house, with everyone cheering and shouting. Those left behind joined the bride inside to set out the food and drinks. They laughed and talked while they waited.

Meanwhile, the men stopped near the foot of a tree that stood at the edge of a small clearing not far into the woods. The surrounding woods were already filling with shadows as the men tied Jeff loosely to a tree. Laughter and music were drifting across the field from the house where the party was getting under way. Figuring Jeff would be back to join the party in around half an hour, the men turned to leave.

"Come on, fellows," Jeff called out. "You can't leave me here like this. You know a bear was spotted in these woods two days ago. Come on. You've had your fun, but it's dangerous. Now untie me!"

The men laughed and ignored him. The farther they walked away from him, the louder Jeff called. They could actually hear fear in his voice now. They were surprised that he was scared. They had heard about the bear sighting, too, but they figured that the animal was just passing through and was long gone by now. They didn't believe for a moment that Jeff was in any danger. They joined the others at the house and took some food and drinks outside to sit in the yard. They were relating how they had tied Jeff up when they were startled to hear terrifying screams from across the field from the clearing. There was no doubt the screams were coming from Jeff.

"Help! Help me!" Jeff yelled as if the cries were being ripped from his throat. "For God's sake, somebody help me!"

The men looked at each other. Jeff was really in trouble! Immediately, without a word, all the men ran through the field to the clearing at the edge of the woods. The screaming stopped before they arrived and, when they looked at the scene before them, they couldn't believe their eyes. What they saw in front of them was unthinkable. Jeff lay perfectly still, mauled and bleeding. A huge bear beside the broken body looked at the men. One man, who always carried a gun, pulled it from his pocket and fired into the air. The men began to shout at the bear until it turned and ran into the woods. They ran to Jeff, but it was too late. He was already dead.

It was one of those things that absolutely couldn't happen; yet it did. The hours and days that followed seemed unreal. The little church where the joyous wedding had taken place such a short time before was now the site of unbearable grief at Jeff's funeral. The day he was laid to rest, the neighbor men tracked and killed the bear.

Nellie moved out of the house that she and Jeff had built with so much love and happy expectations. She lived with her parents for a while, but she couldn't stand it for long. It was too hard to look at the woods and the house and the people. She moved away to live with an aunt in a faraway state. She never came back.

Nobody else moved into the house, and soon it fell to ruin. Nellie's father used it for storage.

People claimed that it wasn't really deserted, though. They claimed that, on the anniversary of the wedding and the chivaree, laughter and singing could be heard at the house. These sounds were followed by heart-wrenching screams coming from the clearing in the woods. Hunters who ventured into the woods on the anniversary night reported that they heard a growl and felt cold chills. They never saw the bear, but they felt its presence stalking them. The sense of danger was so great that they hurried from the woods and never went back at night.

As the years went by, people were so disturbed by the house that Nellie's father eventually tore it down. Those who had to pass by the woods went as quickly as they could. Stories circulated about odd sounds in the clearing and at the spot where the old house used to be. Nobody ventured close enough to check out the sounds, and nobody ever mentioned another chivaree.

Telling the Bees

Tom Simpson, Roberta's father, kept several hives of bees on his farm. He had many bee stories to share. He believed in "telling the bees."

This practice was an odd belief among some communities that may not actually be ghostly, but it definitely falls into the categories of spooky and unexplained. It was said that bees must be told and their hives draped in mourning if the beekeeper or any member of the keeper's family died. If this practice was not carried out, it was believed that the bees would swarm and leave their hives in search of a new home.

It was important in earlier days to have bees on the farm. The honey was used for many things, especially during the Great Depression, when sugar was rationed. Honey was used for such things as healing remedies and for baking. A favorite breakfast treat was hot biscuits, honey, and butter. Naturally, people who kept hives of bees did not want them to swarm and go elsewhere.

Telling the bees was a custom brought over from England and prevailed in New England and the edge of Appalachia. In 1858,

American poet John Greenleaf Whittier even wrote a poem about it called "Telling the Bees." Children read this popular poem in their textbooks at school.

Josh Simms, a Kentucky farmer, always kept several hives of bees at the end of his garden near his barn. He had a remarkable way with the bees that especially impressed his young niece Tina. She noticed that her Uncle Josh never got stung, even when he was taking honey from the hives. The bees would often land on him, but they would fly away without doing him any harm. Then never bothered anyone who was with him, either.

One day Tina and Josh were in the garden gathering vegetables near the beehives. The bees were darting about their heads, but then would fly on.

"Uncle Josh, can you talk to bees?" Tina asked. "Do you tell them not to sting us?"

"Sure, I talk to them," he said, "but not exactly the way I talk to people. I guess they can tell what I'm feeling. They don't sting us because I let them know that we are not going to hurt them."

Tina just smiled. She didn't know if what her uncle said was the truth or just something he made up to tease her.

One day at school, her class read Whittier's poem "Telling the Bees." Tina was fascinated by it, and as soon as she saw her uncle again, she told him about it.

"Uncle Josh," she asked, "do you know that you are supposed to tell the bees if anyone in the family dies?"

"I've heard that," he answered, "and I've read the poem."

"Do you know any beekeepers who told the bees when someone in the family died?" Tina continued.

"Yes," he said. "I had a neighbor once who kept bees. When he died, the family told the bees and draped the hives with strips of black cloth. The bees didn't swarm and leave."

"Do you think they would really swarm and leave if they weren't told?" she said. "Maybe they would have stayed anyway."

He stood looking at his beehives for a minute before he answered.

"I think there is some truth to the custom," he said finally. "I think they would leave if they weren't told. In fact, I saw it happen once when I was a young man, and I'll never forget it. Old man Leach's bees swarmed after he died because nobody told them he was dead."

"How do you know that was why they swarmed?" she asked. "Did you see them leave the hives?"

"No, but I saw where they went. It was really strange, " he said.

"Where did they go?" Tina asked him.

"The Leach family thought the custom of telling the bees about a death was just silly superstition," he told her. "They ignored it and made arrangements for the old man's burial several miles from his home. Most of us in the neighborhood went to the funeral. After the service was finished inside the church, he was carried to the graveyard next to the church, where he was to be buried. A few of us stayed behind after the coffin was lowered into the ground and covered with dirt. People left enough fresh flowers to completely cover the grave, so we placed them over the top.

"Then we heard an odd sound, like a buzzing or humming of some kind. As it got closer and louder, we looked up and saw a dark mass of something approaching from the sky. We were surprised to see that it was a swarm of bees. They landed right on top of Mr. Leach's grave! We stood there and stared in shock for a few seconds, and then we all scattered in every direction."

"Maybe the bees were attracted to the fresh flowers on the grave," Tina suggested.

"Some people thought that," he said. "You know, the unbelievers. But the flowers hadn't been on the grave long enough to attract the bees. The bees had to have started flying before we put the flowers on the grave because the hives were several miles away. Some of us left immediately and went to Mr. Leach's house. We checked the hives, but they were deserted. The bees that came to the graveyard and landed on his grave were his bees. I'll never understand it, but they knew by some unknown means where to find him."

"Would you tell your bees if someone in our family died?" Tina asked.

"Yes, Tina," he answered. "I would definitely tell them."

A few months after this conversation with Tina, Josh learned he had cancer. When he died over a year after that, nobody in the immediate family thought to tell the bees. Tina thought of it during the funeral, and when it was over, she hurried to the hives to check on the bees. They were all gone already. Like their keeper, they had gone to a new home.

The Pie Supper

We were not in our teens yet when pie suppers were popular, so although we never baked any pies for these events, we did share in the pie eating. Miss Mildred, the teacher at the local one-room school, shared a particularly heartbreaking story of one pie supper long ago.

In early times, local churches and schools would hold pie suppers to raise money for the things they needed that did not come under regular budget funds or taxes. In fact, pie suppers provided a major source of funding for many of Kentucky's one-room schools in the late nineteenth and twentieth centuries.

At the pie supper, women and girls would provide their homemade pies to be auctioned off to the highest bidder. The person who bought the pie not only got the pie, but also got to eat it with the pie maker. Pie suppers thus had romantic elements, with young men often competing for a pie.

No names were on the boxes containing the pies, but each box had distinctive decorations. The bidder did not know the identity of the pie maker unless he had some inside information from the girl or her family. Sometimes a girl who liked a certain young man would give him a hint about which box to bid on by secretly revealing some detail about the decorations of her box.

The ladies decorated their pie boxes with ruffles, ribbons, and flowers, mostly made from cloth or crepe paper purchased at the five-and-ten-cent store. Without hints, an element of mystery or surprise was added to the sale. If more than one young man liked the same girl, the competition in bidding would raise the price of the pie beyond the usual cost. Five dollars was considered a high price. Regardless of who purchased the pies, the money went for a good cause and most people had fun. Unfortunately, now and then there would be an exception. One such exception was always remembered.

Fred Doss and Bernice Swanson first met at a pie supper and kept steady company after that. She was sixteen and he was seventeen when it all started, but the romance blossomed and grew for four years. During that time, Houston Holleran had his eye on Bernice, too. Fred always knew (probably with a hint from Bernice) which pie was hers. He always managed to outbid Houston and end up with Bernice.

But the year Fred turned twenty-one was different. He had enlisted in the army and was leaving the day after the pie supper, so it was especially important to Fred and Bernice to share this last pie supper before Fred went off to war. It was equally important to Houston to outbid Fred on this special night. Bernice wanted to make sure Fred bought her pie, so she gave him a big hint.

"My pie box will be decorated in red, white, and blue in honor of your going into the army to serve your country," she said.

Houston figured Bernice would give Fred advance information, so he sent his little sister Alberta over to Bernice's house to spy. Alberta often went to the house to play with Bernice's younger sister, so Bernice thought nothing about the visit. Alberta learned what kind of pie Bernice had baked and even saw the decorated box. This was the information Houston needed. Then Alberta had her mother help her decorate a box that looked like Bernice's box. Alberta changed one tiny detail on the side of the box that nobody but Houston would notice. At the pie supper, Houston placed his sister's box ahead of Bernice's while everybody else was playing games and not paying attention to him. Then he waited.

When the pie auction started, the auctioneer picked up Alberta's box and opened the bidding. Thinking it was Bernice's pie, Fred started to bid. Houston bid against him at first to fool him and to run the bidding up. Then Houston let Fred make the final bid. Fred didn't realize that he had bought the wrong box until Alberta stepped forward and revealed that it was hers. Later, when Bernice's box came up, Fred didn't have enough money left to buy it, so Houston won the bidding with ease.

Everybody thought it was unfair, but the rules of the pie supper were clear. The guy who bought the pie ate the pie with the girl who brought it. On the evening that was supposed to be their own special time, Bernice and Fred had to eat with other people. Houston thought it was hilarious, but the young couple was very disappointed. When Fred walked Bernice home later, she was literally in tears.

"Don't cry," Fred told her. "Houston pulled off a mean trick, but I promise you that no matter what, we'll be together at next year's pie supper!"

Bernice quickly forgot Fred's promise because Fred had

to leave for training the next day. She missed him terribly and refused invitations to go out with Houston. She wrote to Fred every day and prayed every night that he would not have to go overseas to fight. She did not realize that prayers are often answered in ways we do not expect. One day, word came that Fred had been killed in a training accident in boot camp. He would not be going overseas to fight, but he would not be coming home to be with her either. Bernice was devastated. She stayed home and grieved the loss of her sweetheart.

Months passed, and Bernice still refused to attend any social events. Finally, the time came for the annual pie supper. Her parents reminded Bernice that the school needed to raise funds, so she finally agreed to go with them. She covered her box with black crepe paper and added one white rose. Houston decided right away that it was hers, so he bought it when it went up for auction.

Bernice tried to be cheerful afterward while they ate, but Houston knew she was remembering the previous year. Sadness was in her eyes. He felt a twinge of conscience about the way he had acted the year before and tried to make casual conversation. Two other couples joined them and tried to cheer Bernice up.

Suddenly, they heard a noise behind them. It sounded like someone stepping on dry twigs. They all looked around and gasped at what they saw. They couldn't believe their eyes. A figure in an army uniform stood there smiling and gazing at Bernice. There was no doubt about his identity. Fred had clearly kept his promise that they would be together at this pie supper. Bernice fainted and Fred's ghost vanished.

Bernice was never the same after that night. She refused to eat or have visitors. She began to waste away and was dead in a few weeks.

The story goes that as long as they had pie suppers at that school, a ghostly couple could be seen standing off from the crowd. If anyone approached them, they would vanish!

The Whittler's Trail

Some of Russell County's finest whittlers, Mr. Hughes, Mr. Ashbrooks, and Mr. Wilson, gathered on the porch of our little country store and exchanged tales as they whittled. All three could have told this story, but Mr. Wilson probably told it most often. Both the telling and the whittling could be considered art.

Whittling has been around almost as long as mankind itself. It is not a part of Kentucky life now like it used to be, but the tradition is still carried on by some skilled whittlers. In whittling, one cuts or shapes wood, usually into toys, bowls, and the like, using only a knife. The knife is usually a light, small-bladed knife or pocketknife, and the whittler usually whittles objects as a hobby.

In Kentucky up through the 1900s, whittlers could often be seen whittling on the porches of their homes, at the town square, or in front of an old country store. Huley Stanton was one such whittler. He was often seen at Harmon's store, passing the time by creating images of things he saw around him. Cedar wood was mostly his wood of choice because he liked the smell of it.

Five-year-old Danny Peterson loved to accompany his

father, Lee, to the store so he could watch Huley whittle on the porch. Danny was amazed that Huley could pick up a piece of wood and turn it into a gun, animal, doll, or other toy.

"How do you do that?" he'd ask.

"I'll show you when you're a little older," Huley would tell him.

"I don't have a knife," Danny said.

"Well, I'll leave you my knife if anything ever happens to me," Huley promised. "This old knife can just about whittle out things on its own."

Danny didn't want anything to happen to Huley, but he certainly did want a knife of his own like the one Huley had. Whenever he asked for one, though, his parents always told him he was too young. He'd have to wait until he was several years older to get a knife of his own, so Danny had to be satisfied watching Huley use his for now.

Huley and his wife and Danny's family lived in the same neighborhood, but dense woods separated their houses. The woods belonged to Huley, and he often cut and sold timber off his land.

Danny's parents, Hattie and Lee, worked hard on their farm, but they made time to take Danny for walks in the woods. Danny loved all the trees and animals, but he listened to his mom and dad's warning that he must never go into the woods alone. They told Danny that even though the woods held great beauty, they also held great dangers. People in those days made children aware of danger without dwelling on it.

The Petersons lived in a world before security systems,

so, like most people, they secured their doors at night by wooden latches. Danny slept in a small room off the kitchen. Lee and Hattie slept in a large bedroom off the living room. Since there were two rooms between, Lee took special care to secure the latches at night so nothing could get in and Danny would not be able to wander out.

All was well for some time. Then one day, life in the neighborhood started off as usual, but ended up in a way nobody would have expected. The Petersons were working in their garden, and Danny was playing in the yard. In the nearby woods, Huley Stanton went deep among the trees to cut some timber. The Petersons could hear the sound of Huley's axe chopping away. A short time passed with only the axe and the sound of the hoes breaking the silence. Then a crash and a scream rendered the Petersons motionless. Huley's voice was distant, but clear.

"God, help!" he called. "The tree fell on me. It's crushing me. Somebody help me, please!"

They listened for the direction of the sound, but nothing more came.

"Call for help," Lee said to Hattie, as he ran into the woods. Danny started to follow, but his mom held him back.

"Come inside with me," she said. "Your daddy will help Mr. Stanton."

But Huley was beyond help. Other neighbors came to aid Lee, but Huley's injuries were too severe for him to be saved. By the time they were able to remove the tree that was crushing his chest, he was dead.

Danny cried and cried because Huley was gone. He

went to the funeral with his parents, but he wasn't quite sure what being dead really meant. What he did know was that his friend was gone and wouldn't be coming back. When the service was over and everyone went outside, Mrs. Stanton came up to the Petersons to thank them for coming.

"Danny," she said, turning to the boy, "Huley left you something. You may be a little young for it now, but he always told me that he wanted you to have his whittling knife someday. I'll bring it over to you when things settle down a bit."

Her words made Danny feel better. His friend hadn't forgotten his promise!

When they got home, Danny was almost too excited about the knife to eat his supper. His mother urged him to eat because thunder was rumbling in the distance and she wanted to have supper over and the dishes washed before the storm hit.

"Do you think Mrs. Stanton will bring my knife to me tonight?" he asked.

"No," Hattie told her son. "She's too sad now. Besides, a storm is coming."

"But I want my knife now!" Danny insisted.

"Danny, that's enough," his dad told him. "She'll bring it to you when she's ready. You're too little to use it now anyway. You might get hurt."

Danny pouted, but said no more. They finished supper in silence and went to bed before the storm hit.

Danny did not go to sleep, though. He wasn't afraid of

the storm's roaring and lightning. He was thinking about his knife. If Mrs. Stanton didn't want to come through the storm to his house, then he could go to her house. The more he thought about it, the more he thought that this was the thing to do.

He got out of bed quietly and put his clothes on. He tried to release the latch on the kitchen door, but it was too high. He looked around, and his eyes rested on a kitchen chair. He moved it to the door, careful not to wake his parents. They would make him go back to bed. He climbed up on the chair and released the door latch. He didn't think about getting his raincoat. He didn't mind getting wet. It wasn't far to Mrs. Stanton's house anyway. He walked out the door into the woods while his parents slept peacefully inside the house.

Danny hadn't gone far when he began to realize he should not have done this. He knew he was lost. The woods didn't look the same on a stormy night as they did on a sunny day when his mom and dad were with him. He decided to go back home, but when he looked around, he had no idea of where to go. He was already soaked and chilled by the rain, and he wished he had a dry place to sit and rest. He looked around and noticed a large hollow tree standing by the path. He didn't know that hollow trees were dangerous in storms, so he crawled inside the opening in the trunk and rested.

As he sat there, the storm seemed to get a second wind. It blew with fury now, and suddenly a blast of wind uprooted the tree where Danny was resting. Danny tried to hold on, but he bounced back and forth inside the trunk. When the tree came to rest, Danny tried to crawl out, but a large branch pinned him inside. He was alone and lost, and nobody knew where to look for him. He cried and cried, and he thought he heard Huley Stanton tell him he would be all right.

Meanwhile, the renewed energy of the storm woke Hattie Peterson. She heard the kitchen door banging in the wind, so she got out of bed and rushed to the kitchen. One look at the open door sent her hurrying to check on Danny in his room. She knew what she would find. Her son was gone. His bed was empty. She ran into the kitchen.

"Lee, wake up!" she yelled. "Danny's gone!"

Lee pulled on his pants and hurried from the bed to the kitchen. One look at the chair beside the door told him what had happened.

"He's gone after that knife!" he told Hattie. "I've got to go look for him."

"How will you find him in the woods in this storm?" she asked.

The answer to her question came from the darkness outside the door. Lee and Hattie both smelled the strong scent of fresh cedar right outside.

Lee grabbed his coat and lit the lantern. He opened the door, and the light showed a small pile of shavings right there by the door, with a thin trail of shavings leading into the woods. They were cedar shavings like the ones Huley Stanton whittled.

"Wait here," said Lee. "I'll find him now. I have some help!"

Lee followed the trail of shavings into the woods for a few minutes. Then they led him off the main path onto a smaller path that was seldom used. Soon he heard Danny crying.

"Danny!" he called. "Where are you?"

"Here," Danny answered, whimpering now.

The sound was close. Lee looked around, trying to locate the source, when he saw what had happened. He ran over, lifted the limb, and checked Danny for injuries. His ankle was sprained, but otherwise he was unhurt. Just for an instant, Lee felt the presence of Huley Stanton beside him. He breathed a silent thank you to the whittler, picked Danny up in his arms, and carried him home.

Danny had to rest and stay off his ankle for a few days. He was feeling restless and bored one day when his mother came into his room and told him he had a visitor. He was surprised to see Mrs. Stanton.

"I have your knife for you, Danny," she said. "Your mom says you can't use it yet, but I am leaving it with her for you to use later. I brought you something you can use now, though. I found something that Huley whittled, and I know he would want you to have it."

She handed Danny a wooden puzzle that he had seen Huley whittle at Harmon's store. In his mind, Danny could see Huley clearly. It felt like Huley was actually there.

It was many years before Danny used the knife to whittle. Each time he picked up a piece of cedar, he thought of the trail of shavings his dead friend had left that stormy night to save his life.

Burning Tobacco Beds

When we were young, as the time to burn the tobacco beds drew near, we recall hearing warnings to take care to keep the fire from spreading and for everyone to keep away from the flames so our clothes would not catch fire. The Cravens family, the Foley family, and Mr. Bray and his two sons were the ones who usually helped Roberta's dad. One of them told this story one night, but she can't say exactly which one because one story usually followed another, and she was so eager to listen that she did not always notice the transition.

Burning tobacco beds was an event most families enjoyed on the farm, but few people now would remember taking part in it, as it is now part of Kentucky history. Some farmers probably burned tobacco beds well into the 1970s. Up until that time, Kentucky had a lot of burly tobacco growers. Before modern methods took over, farmers grew their tobacco plants in a bed that was 8 feet by 50 feet or 8 by 100. To prepare the beds, they were first burned for weed control.

Long winters often left storm-damaged limbs and brush lying around everywhere. These were gathered, placed in piles, and burned like a huge bonfire over the area where the beds would be. This burning could be a family event or a neighborhood gathering. All help was welcome to carry the limbs and then to watch the fire and keep it from spreading.

The flames from the burning beds always looked spectacular against the early spring night skies. When the flames died out, the farmers raked and spread the ashes and let them cool overnight. Then they mixed the tobacco seeds in the ashes and sowed them in the beds. A cotton cloth was used to cover the beds, and the seeds were left alone to grow. When the seedlings reached a height of eight or ten inches, the farmers transplanted them in the fields. The introduction of methyl bromide and the ability to gas the beds pretty much eliminated the need to burn them. Before that happened, burning tobacco beds occurred every year.

The Grayson family looked forward to tobacco-bed burning each year so they could turn the process into a family bonfire. Faye and her younger sister, four-year-old Ruby Jean, always roasted marshmallows on long sticks as the fire died down. Ruby Jean was fascinated by the flames and loved to stand close and feel the heat on the chilly spring nights. The family constantly had to warn her to stay at a safe distance, but her parents or sister often had to pull Ruby Jean back from the flames.

One night, as the Graysons were burning their tobacco beds, an unexpected wind whipped up the flames. Ruby Jean was standing near the fire when the flames shot out and caught the dress she was wearing. The little girl did the one thing she should never have done. She ran, frightened and screaming, through the field with the wind fanning the flames.

"Drop down and roll," screamed Faye, running after her little sister. "Stop running!"

Mr. and Mrs. Grayson ran after both girls, but by the time Ruby Jean stumbled and fell to the ground, her burns were severe. There were no modern burn units back then, so Ruby Jean died that night.

People in the neighborhood say that the spirit of the little girl lives on, though. They declare that she returns on the anniversary of her death. Some swear that they have heard her scream and that they have looked out the windows to see a fiery light streaking through the field where she was burned. Most people refrained from burning their tobacco beds until that anniversary night had come and gone.

The Graysons never used that field for tobacco beds again. Neighbors said that each year, on the anniversary of that dreadful night, the family would go inside, close the doors and windows, and never look out. It was said that they spent that time praying for the tragic little girl.

Weather Forecaster

There were several teachers in our family and circle of friends. We loved the stories they all told, but Miss Sullivan was a favorite. She had a practice of ending each school day with a story. Storm stories were especially interesting because we had to deal with storms all during the school year. We could relate to these true tales.

In the days of one-room schoolhouses, there were no phones, no radios, and no TV sets in schools to give severe weather alerts. The teacher had to be her own weather forecaster. If a threatening storm approached in the morning, the teacher would keep the students at school and continue with the lessons. She knew that a morning storm was likely to blow itself out by the end of the school day. The little one-room schools were as sturdy as most of the students' homes, so it was safe for them to stay at school until the storm passed. However, if a bad storm approached in the afternoon, the teacher had to consider a different plan of action so her students would not be caught out in the storm.

There were no school buses in those days. All the children lived within walking distance of school, and walked back and forth from home to school every day. The distance might be a mile or more for some children, so the teacher had to take that into consideration when storms were approaching. The storms that came up in early or mid-afternoon would sometimes turn into all-night rains, or at least rain that lasted beyond the regular time for school to be over. The parents and the teacher didn't want students walking home in the storm, so the teacher had to judge whether or not to dismiss school early to allow each child time to reach home safe and dry.

One midafternoon, a particularly bad-looking cloud loomed up without much warning. The teacher looked out the window and decided that, unless they all wanted to be stuck at school until after dark, she should let the students go home immediately.

"Boys and girls," she said, "I want you to listen to me carefully. A very bad cloud is moving this way. I believe you can get home before this storm hits, but you must hurry as fast as you can. Get your things now and run. Don't stop to play. Hurry!"

The students grabbed their books and lunch buckets (yes, buckets, because most students carried their food to school in little buckets that originally contained syrup), rushed out the door, and scattered in all directions. The teacher picked up her purse and some papers to grade that night and headed home herself, leaving the schoolhouse door unlocked as she always did.

One little boy had just reached the dirt road that led through the fields to his house when he realized he had left his arithmetic book at school. He had been having trouble with fractions, and his father had insisted that he bring the book home every night so they could study together. He didn't want his father to be angry, so he stopped and thought about what to do.

He looked at the darkening sky, but the main cloud still seemed to be in the distance. He knew the teacher always left the door unlocked for students who arrived early in the morning, so he decided he would go back. He hurried back to school, ran inside, snatched up the book, closed the door behind him, and dashed off for home as fast as he could.

Unfortunately, the little fellow misjudged the storm's speed. By now the storm had reached the boy, and the wind was whipping the limbs of the trees up and down furiously. He felt the cloud open up and saw a wall of rain heading right toward him. He clutched his book and wondered how he could keep it dry in the downpour. Just then he passed a hollow tree standing by the side of the road. The rain had reached him now, so he squeezed himself and his book into the huge hollow trunk.

The boy had been warned about trees like this. They were called widow makers because they often blew down in storms and killed the men who took shelter in them, leaving their wives widows. He did not heed the warning that day. He only thought of shelter from the storm, and that tree offered the only shelter available. The situation quickly turned tragic. A blast of wind uprooted the tree, crushing the little boy beneath the trunk as it fell.

The unbearable pain he was feeling brought darkness, so the boy wasn't aware that the storm soon stopped and that his father and his neighbors were looking for him. He lived long enough for them to find him and for him to tell them why he had gone back to school. He never knew that his arithmetic book had somehow remained dry and undamaged.

School was dismissed for the boy's funeral. When classes resumed, the teacher and the students missed the boy very much. They thought of him every day when they looked at his empty desk. The days came and went.

Then one day another storm headed for the school. The teacher was trying to decide if she should let the children leave when a student gasped, "Look!"

Everybody looked to where the boy was pointing. There stood the ghost of the little boy with his book under his arm, pointing toward the door.

The teacher took that as a sign that the storm was going to be bad and that they should all hurry home. She told the students to go. Remembering the fate of their former schoolmate, they wasted no time getting home. It turned out to be one of the worst storms of the year, but they felt that the ghost boy had saved them.

Until the school burned down mysteriously in a storm

a year later, the ghost boy became a dependable weather forecaster. He didn't come in ordinary rain, but he always appeared if a storm was going to be dangerous.

Turkey Drive

Stories about cattle drives are common in the history of our country, but stories of turkey drives are rare. We were lucky to hear the personal stories of our grandfathers, Louis Franklin Simpson and James Milton Rooks, who participated in some of the drives.

Milton said that the turkeys sometimes had their own ideas about where they wanted to go. The men would take the family dog along to help control the turkeys, but it wasn't much help. The gobblers would spread their tails and fluff up their feathers to look bigger, and the dog would be intimidated and just stand and bark.

When the turkey drovers were settled at their campsite for the night, Lewis Simpson would lead them in an evening of music, storytelling, and fun. He passed on one of those stories to us.

Turkey drives took place in the nineteenth century in the Midwest, the South, and even New England. Basically, cattle drives and turkey drives were the same. They were intended to get the livestock to market, and the journey was sometimes long and difficult. Louis always felt that turkey drives were more difficult than cattle drives. The cattle might become spooked and scatter in all directions, but they always stayed at ground level with the drovers, so they could be reached and rounded up. That was not the case with turkeys.

According to Louis, the turkeys were harder to control. They might be spooked by anything. Howling or barking dogs, rifle shots, paper blowing in the wind, or unseen things like engines or people talking often made the turkeys take flight. They might end up on the tops of buildings or in trees, out of reach of the drovers. At that point, the turkeys were in charge. It was often impossible for the drovers to coax them down to continue on their way. Most of the time, the drovers simply set up camp where the turkeys had chosen to roost or take refuge from whatever frightened them.

The turkeys usually lived off the land, enjoying a diet of grasshoppers, nuts, plants, and the like. Drovers sometimes brought along a wagon filled with shelled corn, just in case the land did not provide food.

One late afternoon, a turkey drive approached a small town in south central Kentucky. Louis Simpson's old bluetick hound was taking a nap when he was disturbed by the drovers herding the turkeys down the road. He sat up and gave a couple of sharp, loud barks before deciding that this matter did not really require his attention. He lay back to continue his nap, but the turkeys flew into the highest tree seeking safety.

A boy who lived in town had heard that the turkey drive was coming through. He had never shot a turkey, and he decided it would be a good time to try out his new twenty-two rifle. This could be his lucky day. His luck held as he sneaked the rifle out of the house and hid in the bushes along the road. His luck continued to run as he heard the dog bark and the turkeys fly to safety in the treetops. It deserted him completely, however, when he failed to notice one of the drovers climbing up a tree to try to scare the turkeys down.

The boy raised his rifle and sighted only the turkey. It was a big one that would win him a lot of admiration among his friends if he could shoot it. Behind the tree, the drover climbed swiftly and silently, out of the boy's line of vision. Two things happened at the same time. The young drover leaned around the tree and reached for the turkey. The young boy on the ground pulled the trigger and sent a bullet into the drover's head. The horrified boy watched as the drover's body fell to the ground with a thud. The turkey they'd both been after fled to another tree and was later caught and sold at market.

The shooter, who was a minor, was not jailed as an adult. He was sent away to a reform school up north, and the victim was sent to the cemetery. That was not the end of it, though. On the anniversary of that tragic incident, people heard the sound of wings in the trees. They heard a single shot and the thud of a body hitting the ground. They always looked, but nothing was there. The scene was destined to be replayed over and over for many years until finally the sounds got fainter and fainter and disappeared altogether.

Fool's Errand

The hunters in our community told this story. With little to do for entertainment when they were camped for the night on a hunting trip, they would resort to practical jokes to have some laughs. When they gathered at our home or the home of neighbors, they would recount their escapades. Most were innocent fun, but this one joke, which always stayed in our minds, had a terrible ending.

A fool's errand is sometimes also called a snipe hunt or a wild-goose chase. In early times in Kentucky and the southern United States, it was a type of practical joke that involved experienced people making fun of inexperienced people by setting them up with an impossible or imaginary task. Campers and hunters often practiced this kind of prank. The victim of the joke had to do silly or preposterous things to complete the task, but of course doing so was hopeless. The fool's errand came in two varieties: trying to find something that does not exist, or trying to accomplish an impossible task.

Many years ago, a group of hunters had pitched camp deep in the woods. After eating their dinner, cooked over an open fire, they were bored and looking for entertainment.

In the group was a young man named Ronald Wilson, who was on his first hunt. His presence made the opportunity for a fool's errand too good to pass up.

The group had considered a snipe hunt, but they discarded that idea because Ronald knew there really was such a thing as a snipe—it was a real bird that was very hard to catch. The group wanted something unreal and a whole lot scarier than a snipe. Finally, they came up with the idea of an imaginary monster called a Swamp Booger. Now that dinner was over, they were ready to put their plan into action.

"Boys, how would you like to catch a Swamp Booger tonight?" one hunter asked in mock seriousness.

"Naw, no way!" the others answered as planned.

"Ronald, how would you like to catch one?" the first hunter asked.

Ronald shifted uneasily on the ground and looked at the group.

"I never heard of a Swamp Booger," he laughed nervously.

"Well, we've all seen it and had a crack at it," said the hunter, "but none of us could catch it. You might just be the man to do the job!"

Ronald was tired from the day's hunt, and he didn't feel like hunting anything else that night. He did swell up a little with pride at being referred to as a man. All he really wanted, though, was to stretch out and go to sleep. It was obvious that this was not what his companions had in mind.

"What do you say?" the hunter persisted. "You up to giving it a try?"

All eyes were on Ronald, intent on their purpose of getting him to agree. He felt trapped and uneasy.

"I don't know," he said. "What would I have to do?"

That was all the encouragement they needed. They all immediately moved closer to give him instructions.

"It's attracted by sounds," one hunter said. "You have to beat two rocks together and call softly, 'Swamp Booger! Swamp Booger!'"

"It may take a few minutes, but you will hear it coming," said another. "It drags its tail and growls a low growl just before it attacks. Don't let it get too close. It has paws with three claws only. You have to shoot when you hear the growl so it won't claw you to death."

That didn't sound too inviting to Ronald.

"Why can't we all go hunt it together?" he asked.

"Oh, it won't show itself if it hears more than one person," said a third hunter. "We'll all hide nearby and be quiet, but you have to go out and call it by yourself."

"I wish I could catch it," said the first hunter, "but it's too quick for a man my age. The man that brings it in will be a real hero! I wish it could be me!"

Suddenly, Ronald was caught up in the action by the idea of being a hero.

"Okay, I'll give it shot," he told them.

One hunter handed him two rocks. Another passed him his gun. They helped him to his feet and pushed him along into the dark woods beyond the firelight.

They stopped and Ronald stumbled along alone, beating the rocks together. His self-confidence rose a little as he moved ahead. Maybe he really could catch this thing. It would be a great feeling to outdo the others. His walk was steadier now.

"Swamp Booger! Swamp Booger!" he called softly.

Back at the campfire, the hunters rolled on the ground laughing. They could hardly believe that anyone would really be dumb enough to think there was a real thing called a Swamp Booger.

They heard Ronald move farther into the woods. They followed at a safe distance so Ronald would not discover them.

"Swamp Booger! Swamp Booger!" Ronald kept calling.

Then suddenly they all heard something they were

not supposed to hear. Something was dragging through the woods. Then it was growling!

The hunters heard the rocks go silent. A single shot rang out. The sounds that followed were terrifying. Ronald was screaming and struggling as the growling got louder. Then there was silence for just a minute. The hunters stood, unable to move, as they heard a dragging sound going in the opposite direction into the woods. They hurried to see what had happened to Ronald. It was horrible—and no longer a joke.

Ronald lay dead on the ground. His face had three claw marks. His gun had been fired once. The rocks were covered with blood, as if he had tried to use them to defend himself. Signs were evident that something like a tail had been dragged along the ground.

Ronald's death was ruled as "death by an unknown animal attack."

The hunters thought about it over and over in the next year. Of course there was no such beast as the one they had described to Ronald. It was just a coincidence that some animal had come out of the woods and killed him. They put it out of their minds and went on their annual hunt. Nobody mentioned the fool's errand they had sent Ronald on the year before.

They sat around the fire and ate their supper. They were thinking about turning in for the night when faint sounds came from the woods. The sounds came closer and closer, and the hunters realized they were hearing the sound of someone beating two rocks together.

"Swamp Booger! Swamp Booger!" a voice called softly.

The frightened men dashed water on the fire, grabbed their gear, and loaded it on their truck. They drove as fast as they could and never looked back. Their hunting consisted of day trips from then on. None of them was foolish enough to go back into the woods at night again.

Rest for the Traveler

We travel a lot with our book signings and storytelling, and we take for granted the reserved room at a hotel or motel, hot food and hot showers, and the privacy of a room to ourselves where we can rest and feel safe. We live across the street from a historic inn, which gives us an idea of how it must have been long ago. There are lots of tales about peddlers and old inns, but this one illustrates the conditions we imagine.

In the old days, hotels and motels did not dot the landscape of our country like they do now. Now when we travel, we take these luxuries for granted, but this was not always the case. In early times, traveling salesmen (or peddlers, as they were often called) could not call ahead and reserve a room for the night. They had to depend on the hospitality of people who lived along the route they traveled to put them up for the night. This practice usually worked out well for all concerned. People living far from town welcomed a chance to buy things they needed from the peddlers, and they enjoyed the company and the news that the peddler passed on. The peddlers appreciated the food and a place to sleep, whether it would be a bed inside the house or a bed in the hay in the barn.

Naturally, there could be complications. Sometimes a peddler would encounter an unscrupulous host who would notice the peddler's money from prior sales. After offering the peddler a bed, the greedy host would wait until everyone was asleep and take action. He would kill and rob the unsuspecting peddler and dispose of the body somewhere nearby. Since there were no records of these travelers, the murderer would say that the peddler had left early or maybe never came by at all. Such disappearances were rarely pursued or solved.

The large farmhouse set among the trees was a happy sight for the peddler. He had done well so far, but he was getting too tired to go on to the next town. He stopped and showed his wares to the occupants of the house, and was pleased with his sales there. When his host extended an invitation for him to spend the night, the peddler gladly accepted the offer. He was especially happy to have shelter that night because a nasty storm was brewing, and he didn't want to be caught in it trying to get to the next town.

The farmer's wife hurried to get supper on the table before the storm hit. She didn't like having her hands in dishwater when lightning was in the air for fear it would shock or strike her. She was relieved that they finished dinner and the dishes just as the storm arrived in full force. The lightning danced on the rooftop, and the rain poured down in sheets.

It was a great night for sleeping, so they all retired early. The farmer's wife made a pallet for the peddler on the floor in front of the fireplace. He placed his pack beside him on the floor. The farmer had seen quite a lot of money in it when he paid him earlier.

"You should rest well here," said the farmer. "We will try not to disturb you, but my wife will insist that we go to the cellar if the storm gets worse. She is afraid of storms."

The peddler assured the farmer that he would be fine. They said goodnight, and all went to sleep except the farmer. He lay awake thinking about all the money the peddler was carrying.

That money would pay off all my debts if I had it, he thought. A wicked plan began to form in his mind.

While the storm continued, the farmer slipped out of bed and crept into the living room. The peddler was sleeping peacefully on the floor, his pack beside him. If he heard the farmer's footsteps, he probably thought it was the family going to the cellar. The peddler's rest was undisturbed until the farmer picked up the poker and bashed in his head with one blow.

With his actions covered by the noise of the storm, the farmer dragged the peddler's body to the cellar. He hid it in an old rug, knowing it would not be discovered until he could take it out and bury it later. He made a second trip to get the peddler's pack with his goods and money, and hid the pack in a trunk in the corner of the cellar. He cleaned the poker and went back to bed. Sometime before dawn, the storm moved on.

The next morning, the farmer's wife was surprised to find the peddler gone. She had expected him to stay for breakfast.

"Where is he?" she asked.

"He left as soon as the storm let up," her husband told her. "He said he wanted to get an early start."

She knew that peddlers did want to get an early start sometimes, so she thought no more about it. Soon after, while the wife and children were visiting neighbors, the farmer took the body and the trunk with the money out of his cellar and buried them where only he would know where to look. He figured he could get whatever amount of money he needed from the trunk when he needed it.

The farmer was shrewd enough not to pay off all his debts at once. He did not want to make anyone suspicious. He justified his killing the peddler by telling himself over and over that he had worked hard all his life and deserved some good luck, even if he had to create it for himself. Now all he had to do was wait and spend the money a little at a time. Nobody would suspect a thing. He would not have to pay for this crime.

Some time later, another storm came up right after supper. There was no guest that night, but the family ate early and went to bed as they had done before. The farmer's wife was just dozing off when she heard noises in the living room. She heard footsteps, a thud, and the sound of something being dragged to the cellar. She gave her husband a shake.

"Wake up!" she said. "Somebody is in the house."

"It's just the storm," he told her.

"No!" she insisted. "I heard something inside!"

Just to satisfy his wife, he got out of bed and went into the living room.

"Nothing's in here!" he called.

"Check the cellar," she told him.

She heard her husband open the cellar door, and then she heard him scream! She sat up in bed as she heard what sounded like an inert body thumping from step to step to the bottom of the stairs. Her children were out of bed now and joined her as she hurried down to where the farmer's body lay. Nobody knows what he saw, but the look of fright on his face sent the wife and children running up the stairs to send for the sheriff.

The sheriff concluded that the farmer had tripped accidentally on the stairs and fallen to his death. He saw no reason to search the cellar.

The family tried to stay on in the house, but on stormy nights strange sounds kept them awake. They searched, but they could never find the source. Finally, they had to move away. Others bought the house and heard the same noises. One farmer plowing the field near the barn turned up the remains of a man and a trunk filled with money. The sheriff had no proof, but it was evident what had happened. Nobody wanted to live there after that, so the house was eventually torn down.

Since the peddler was never given a proper burial, some wonder if his ghost is still out there somewhere on stormy nights, hoping someone will help him find eternal rest.

Stories from Headlines

Our families were very interested in the news they heard. We did not get daily or weekly newspapers, but our relatives in cities would sometimes send us newspapers or articles. Discussion of a particularly dramatic story would go on and on. There are so many stories on TV, computers, or in newspapers and magazines today that any one story does not remain as popular. New stories come along so fast that a story that captures the imagination one day is replaced by another the next day.

Some of the best stories passed on to us were those that the tellers learned from headlines and news articles. We didn't often see these sources ourselves; some of these stories happened before we were born. In this section we re-tell stories that intrigued friends or family enough that they read them and passed them on in their own words. Some of the original news articles may still be found in newspaper archives or on the Internet. To find them, just type the subject of the story into your computer and search the Internet.

The Ghost of Floyd Collins

*A Kentucky death that made national headlines back in the 1920s
was the death of Floyd Collins. Sand Cave in the Mammoth Cave
area of central Kentucky is said to be haunted by Collins, an explorer
who was trapped and died in the cave in 1925. This was exciting
news to our families because it happened not too far away from us.
We had relatives in the area. Thus, the story of Floyd Collins was
close to our community and our hearts.*

*The Collins family owned Crystal Cave near Mammoth Cave.
Crystal Cave was beautiful, but it attracted few tourists because of
its isolated location. The owners of the various caves in the vicinity competed for tourists in those days, and Collins wanted to find
another entrance to the underground cave system that might result
in more tourists visiting his family's cave.*

*For three weeks, Floyd Collins worked on his plan to find an
entrance or connection. During that time, he worked alone, exploring and expanding a hole that the news media would later call "Sand
Cave."*

Collins worked a few hours in Sand Cave on January 30, 1925,
and managed to squeeze through some narrow passageways
that he claimed led to a large chamber. His lamp was dying,
so he decided to leave before exploring this chamber.

As he was leaving, Collins accidentally knocked over
his lamp, extinguishing his light. That made his attempted
departure even more difficult. Unable to see where he was
going, he dislodged a rock from the ceiling, pinning his left

leg and making it impossible for him to get out. Later, it was determined that the rock weighed only 26½ pounds, but the way it was lodged prevented him and his rescuers from reaching it. It was also discovered later that he was trapped just 150 feet from the entrance to the cave and 55 feet below the surface.

When Collins didn't come home, friends searched and found him the next day. They took him hot food and ran an electric lightbulb down into the passage to give him some light and warmth. Rescue efforts were started, but the unstable passage collapsed in two places on February 4. This eliminated his food and water supply and all contact except by voice. The rescuers believed the cave to be dangerous and impassable at this point, so they began to dig an artificial shaft and lateral tunnel in an attempt to reach Floyd through another chamber. Their efforts failed, but they kept trying to find something that would work.

Soon the life-threatening predicament of Floyd Collins caught the attention of the media, and people came from all over the country to visit the site where Floyd was trapped. A kind of carnival-like atmosphere took over as Floyd was trapped and dying. His own family is said to have made a nice amount of money from selling Floyd Collins souvenirs. Reporters sent stories to their papers across the country, and everybody waited and prayed for his rescue. Tragically, that was not to be. Rescuers finally reached him on February 17, but by then he was dead from exposure, thirst, and starvation.

At that point, rescuers decided that it was too dangerous

to attempt to remove the body, so they left it as they found it and filled up the shaft with debris. Later, a doctor estimated that Floyd had died three or four days earlier, probably on February 13.

A funeral service was held for Floyd Collins on the surface of the cave, but this did not seem right to his brother Homer. Sand Cave did not seem to Homer Collins like a proper resting place for his brother, even though notable explorers in Europe were often buried in the caves they discovered. Two months later, Homer and some friends reopened the shaft, dug a new tunnel, and were finally able to remove Floyd's body on April 23, 1925. On April 26, Floyd's body was buried on the Collins homestead near Crystal Cave. Later the cave would be renamed Floyd Collins Crystal Cave in his honor. It seemed that Floyd would finally be able to rest in peace, but stories about him tell us that his rest was not for long.

In 1927, Floyd's father, Lee Collins, sold the homestead, along with Floyd's grave and Crystal Cave. By June 13, the new owner had thought of a wonderful tourist attraction. He had Floyd's body placed in a glass-topped coffin and exhibited it for many years at the entrance to Crystal Cave. People say it was a profitable move because many people came and paid to gawk at a man who had become a legend.

Later, other stories circulated. As if it were not disturbing enough for people to pay to look at this unfortunate man, someone stole his body on the night of March 18–19, 1929. Some people thought the owners of the property might have done it for publicity to increase tourist interest, but they had no proof. Others thought it was a prank, but nobody ever knew for sure. The body was soon recovered not far from the cave, but Floyd's left leg was missing. The leg was never found.

After this theft, the body was kept in a chained casket in a secluded section of Crystal Cave. Most of the family had long objected to Floyd's casket being placed in the cave for public viewing.

In 1961, Crystal Cave was purchased by Mammoth Cave National Park and officials closed it to the public. At the request of the Collins family, the National Park Service removed Floyd's body and interred it in the Flint Ridge Cemetery on March 4, 1989. It took a team of fifteen men three days to remove the casket and tombstone from Crystal Cave and take it to its final resting place.

After the long ordeal of his stay in the cave both in life and death, Floyd Collins's spirit may feel more at home there than in Flint Ridge Cemetery. Some people have reported hearing a weak voice in the cave calling for help. Others claim to have seen him standing in the cave. Perhaps he is looking for his lost leg. True or not, the elements are there for the ghost of the fallen hero to return.

Kentucky's Killer Ghost

Two questions often come up in discussions about ghosts. "Are there evil ghosts?" and "Do they ever kill? " We rarely encounter stories that say yes to either question, but Kentucky folklore does have one such story, about a man named Carl Pruitt. Troy Taylor, our good friend and renowned author of many books on the paranormal, has written about this case in his book Beyond the Grave. *His version is our favorite. Other renditions of the story may be found in the late Michael Paul Henson's book* More Kentucky Ghost Stories, *as well as on the Internet.*

Our story begins in eastern Kentucky in June 1938. Carl Pruitt came home from work and discovered his wife in bed with another man. The cowardly lover escaped through a window, leaving the wife to face the wrath of her husband alone. He was so enraged that he strangled her with a small piece of chain. When his rage subsided and he realized what he had done, he committed suicide by shooting himself. Police considered it a clear case of murder-suicide and closed the case. It was not over, however. In fact, it was just the beginning.

Carl and his wife were buried in separate cemeteries. Unfortunately, no pictures of the graves are available. She evidently rested in eternal peace, but Carl's rage apparently lived on. A few weeks after he was buried, people began to notice the pattern of a chain forming on his gravestone. A discoloration in the stone kept growing until it formed a small-linked chain that twisted back on itself to form a cross. It frightened the local residents so much that they wanted to remove the stone. Officials refused to let them do it, but they remained uneasy.

Something about this strange occurrence seemed evil to

those who saw it. Most people chose to stay away from the grave and leave Carl Pruitt alone. Of course, there were a few who didn't, and they paid dearly for it.

About a month after the image on the stone stopped growing, a group of local teenagers decided to ride their bicycles through the cemetery where Carl Pruitt was buried. One boy decided to defy the warnings of people who said evil was associated with the stone and that it was dangerous to disturb it. He stopped and threw rocks at the gravestone, knocking several large chips out of it. Laughing, yet a little frightened now that one of the group had actually caused minor damage to the stone, the teenagers all pedaled away toward their homes.

Suddenly, a strange thing happened to the boy who did the damage. His bicycle began to speed out of control, and he couldn't stop it. It veered off the road and crashed into a tree. Then the unbelievable happened. The sprocket chain tore loose, wrapped itself around the boy's neck, and strangled him to death. Even more unbelievable, the day after the boy's death, the tombstone was completely whole again. The pieces he had knocked off were back on again!

The dead boy's mother was distraught after his death. During the next month, her grief and anger built until she couldn't stand it anymore. She had to have revenge. She took a small hand axe to the graveyard and pounded Carl Pruitt's tombstone into a dozen pieces. Then she went back home, feeling some relief after what she had done. The next day, she did the family wash and took the clothes out to the yard to hang them on her clothesline to dry. Most clotheslines were made of rope or wire, but hers was made of a small chain. While she was hanging the clothes, she somehow stumbled and became entangled in the clothesline. She was strangled to death trying to get free. After she died, the Pruitt tombstone she had smashed with her axe miraculously became whole, just as it had done once before.

As news of these strange deaths spread, a morbid interest in the tombstone grew. There were those who believed and stayed at a respectful distance, but there were those who disbelieved and wanted to prove the believers wrong.

A short time passed, and one day a farmer and three members of his family were driving by the cemetery where Pruitt was buried. The farmer was one of the skeptics and likely wanted to prove something to his family members. He pulled out a gun he always carried and fired several shots at Pruitt's headstone. He hit his target, and chunks of the headstone flew in all directions. Frightened by the shots, the horses ran faster and faster until the wagon was out of control. The family members jumped to safety, but the farmer held on, pulling the reins to stop. His efforts were useless, and the wagon swerved around a curve, throwing the farmer from his seat. He flew forward and caught on one of the trace chains, breaking his neck. Once again, after this tragic event, Carl Pruitt's tombstone was whole again!

Talk of curses and mysterious deaths grew in the community and was called to the attention of the local congressman. He felt compelled to respond, so he sent two police officers to the cemetery to investigate the odd stories. One of the officers considered the assignment somewhat beneath him, so he laughed and joked about ghosts and curses. He and his partner took some photos and left to interview some witnesses to the events. As they were leaving in the police car, the skeptical officer saw a light coming from the direction of Carl Pruitt's headstone. As it came closer and closer, the officer drove faster and faster. As it reached the car, the officer swerved off the road and crashed the car between two posts. He was hit by a chain that had been hanging between the two posts. It smashed through the windshield, wrapped around the officer's neck, and almost severed his head. The other officer was thrown free and injured only slightly.

The officer's death was enough to make most people believers and to keep them away from the cemetery. There was one unfortunate exception, however; his name was Mr. Lewis. He declared the whole thing was nonsense and set out one night with a chisel and sledgehammer to prove it. People in the vicinity of the cemetery could hear the sounds as he chipped away at the stone, but they kept their distance and did nothing until they heard a blood-curdling scream cut through the night air. Several men grabbed lanterns and hurried to the cemetery to see what had happened. When they reached the gate, they found Mr. Lewis dead there, looking as though he had been running to escape. The long chain used to keep the gate closed was wrapped around his neck. They figured that he must have been so frightened by something that he forgot about the chain and ran right into it. The strange thing was that all the hammering he did on Pruitt's stone did no damage to it at all.

This last death convinced people to stay away. Many bodies were removed and reburied at other locations because nobody wanted to visit their loved ones with Carl Pruitt nearby. Eventually, Pruitt's grave became overgrown with weeds. He and his wife were childless, so there was nobody to tend the grave. In 1958, a strip-mining operation covered the grave and the body forever.

Was Carl Pruitt really an evil ghost who reached out and killed the people who disturbed or mocked him? We will never know for sure, but we do know that these stories persist. There is enough evidence to convince many people that some spirits are not to be laughed at or bothered.

The Ghost of Cumberland Falls

We especially love stories from towns near us. Relatives in Somerset told us of a haunted place nearby.

Cumberland Falls State Park, located in the Daniel Boone National Forest in eastern Kentucky, draws more visitors than any other park in the state. It's known as the Niagara of the South because of the 125-foot-wide falls that plunge 60 feet into a gorge below, which makes it the second largest waterfall in North America. It also has the Western Hemisphere's only Moonbow, a phenomenon that occurs on a clear night with a full moon by the mist of the falls. With such magic, Cumberland Falls naturally has its share of legends and ghost stories.

A favorite ghost story of the area dates back to the 1950s. Like many young couples, a bride and groom came to Cumberland Falls State Park for their honeymoon. With so many wonderful things to see in the park, the couple decided to visit all the sites in the park before going back to their room in the lodge.

There were many spectacular views that they wanted to remember, so they took lots of pictures to put in their album later. They especially wanted to get some shots with the falls in the background. After a short search, they found an overlook just a few hundred feet from the falls that would work perfectly for the photos they wanted.

The groom wanted to get some shots of his beautiful bride first, so he selected a spot for her to pose. At his direction, she moved to a position on the Pillars, a spot at the edge of a 75- to 80-foot cliff. In the excitement of posing for him, the young woman unknowingly moved too close to the edge. Suddenly, she lost her balance and fell to her death below. The place where this terrible tragedy happened is now known as "Lovers' Leap."

Since this fatal accident, there have been many reports of sightings of the ghostly bride. Sometimes she is spotted on the bridge. Some people report that they are driving around the last curve before the site of her accident and they hit a woman in a wedding dress. When they stop to look for her, she is gone. But evidently, she doesn't stay gone. She returns again and again to the place she was supposed to experience her greatest happiness. Maybe she hopes that on one of her ghostly visits, things will go as they should have done back in the 1950s.

Ashland's Paramount Art Center Ghost

The story of the Paramount Art Center came to our attention a few years ago while we were telling stories in eastern Kentucky. Members of the audience at the college library shared it with us.

The art center, which is listed in the National Register of Historic Places, was originally planned as a theater called the Paramount Center in Ashland, Kentucky. Plans called for it to be three times its current size, but construction plans were cancelled because of the Great Depression. An Ashland-based company scaled down the plans and built it anyway. The Paramount Center opened on September 5, 1931.

The ghostly action at the Paramount started during its construction. The crew members went on their usual lunch break one day, but one of the workers, a man named Joe, chose to stay behind to finish up some work. When the crew returned from lunch, they were shocked to find Joe's body in the auditorium, hanging from the curtain rigging above the stage. No one has determined whether his death was an accident or a suicide. Since his death, Joe has remained in the theater in ghostly form.

Joe's ghost has been seen on a few occasions, but mainly he prefers to be heard and felt rather than seen. He is believed to be responsible when things go missing, when the lights go off and on mysteriously, when cold spots appear and disappear, and when unexplained noises are heard. He is friendly, though, and sometimes helps by opening doors when he is asked.

The most publicized account of Joe's presence happened in 1992 when singer Billy Ray Cyrus was filming his "Achy, Breaky Heart" video at the Paramount Center. He signed eight-by-ten photographs of himself for each of the female staff members as well as a special one made out to "Paramount Joe." These photos hung in the box office until the walls got so crowded with other pictures that the executive director asked the women to take some down. They only removed the photo addressed to Joe. They soon learned that this was definitely the wrong thing to do.

The next morning when they came to work, they discovered that all of Billy Ray's signed pictures had been knocked from the wall! They got the message and immediately hung the picture signed to Joe back in its own special place on the wall.

Another story tells of Joe's ghost turning on lights for two recently hired employees who went to the basement by themselves to check on some old items of interest. They were very grateful since they did not know where the light switches were. They thought the marketing director had done it, but, when they checked, they learned he couldn't have done it because he had been talking on the phone. They gave Joe credit for his help.

In 2004, a local psychic called the marketing director and told him she had a message for him from the other side.

Surprised, he asked, "What is it?"

"I am supposed to tell you that Joe said he is still here," she said.

The theater is now a nonprofit organization where plays, symphonies, and ballets are held. If you should decide to pay a visit to Joe's favorite hangout, chances are that Joe will be there from the other side to meet and greet you.

The Tumbling Tombstone

For many years, people who came and went in our storytelling circle of friends told about a strange, unlikely happening in Bardstown, Kentucky.

Bardstown has more than its share of intriguing ghosts and haunted places. Haunted inns and haunted jails draw tourists to investigate and enjoy ghost walks. A particularly fascinating paranormal happening in this historic town concerns the story told in our circle about a tombstone placed at the head of John Rowan's grave that refuses to stay in place.

John Rowan was one of Kentucky's most important and impressive politicians. He was a state judge, served seven terms in the legislature, and was a U.S. senator, Kentucky secretary of state, and chief justice for the Court of Appeals.

He was also a cousin of Stephen Foster, who wrote "My Old Kentucky Home" after visiting Rowan's mansion, Federal Hill. The stately mansion was deeded to Rowan and his wife by his wife's father as a wedding gift and was a perfect home for the Rowans' impressive way of life.

John Rowan had an unimpressive beginning, though. He was such a sickly child that his family never expected him to live to adulthood. His father moved the family to Kentucky, where young John thrived in the fresh air. He became a brilliant scholar, started his career as a lawyer, and married a woman named Ann Lytle. They entertained many dignitaries at their Federal Hill home.

John Rowan died July 13, 1843. Before his death, he made it clear that he did not want any stone marker or monument erected over his grave. Since his parents had never had markers, he felt it would be disrespectful to them if he had a marker for himself. He thought his home and his life were tributes enough to him and that he needed no monuments.

Rowan was buried first in the Bardstown Cemetery. Somehow, this site did not seem right for such a prominent man. The family thought about it and decided shortly after his burial to remove him from the Bardstown Cemetery and relocate him in the Rowan family cemetery, which was called Federal Hill Cemetery. They also decided to ignore his wishes about having no headstone. They erected a tall obelisk in his honor. Though it was beautiful and tasteful, it must not have pleased Rowan.

Just a few days after the installation of the obelisk, the monument tumbled over for no apparent reason. At that point, of course, stories began to spread about how strange it was that Rowan's wishes had been disregarded and now the stone had mysteriously fallen. Stonemasons were called in to fix the monument. They did not think it was a mystery. They blamed tree roots and settling ground for the monument's fall.

The mystery was not solved by their answer. In less than two months, the monument had tumbled over again. Stonemasons were called in again to repair it, but this time they expressed no opinion on the cause of the fall. Stories continued to circulate that John Rowan's spirit was not happy with that monument. More and more people accepted this story as true when the monument fell yet again shortly after the stonemasons had repaired it. This time, it landed directly on John Rowan's grave. That did it! The stonemasons refused to work on the monument again.

Cemetery caretakers took over the responsibility of repairing the stone and keeping it upright. Rumor has it that they still have to deal with this problem. No one knows the reason for the repeated falls, but everyone in that area seems to think it is a sign that Rowan meant what he said about not wanting a monument or stone marker at his grave. His spirit is apparently angry because his wishes were not carried out.

The Nannie Womack and Elmer Hill Hauntings

The facts of what has been called "Russell County's crime of the century" may never be sorted out completely. When we were growing up in Russell County, the story was only repeated to us in hushed tones. One of Elmer Hill's supposedly intended victims who got away was a teacher who never spoke to us about it. Yet several versions of the brutal slaying and raping of young Nannie Womack and the subsequent hanging of Elmer Hill keep popping up after all these years. Since the case was never brought to trial, all the facts may not be in these accounts.

The late Brother Morris Gaskins of Russell Springs, Kentucky, wrote one account based on newspaper stories and interviews with local citizens. Editors of Adair County and Russell County papers and other regional papers wrote articles full of valuable information. Relatives wrote accounts, too, giving additional information. The account here is the one we heard most often.

The crime occurred on December 8, 1908, and the victim was a young schoolgirl. Nannie Womack's age is variously given as nine, ten, eleven, and even twelve years old, but her tombstone shows she was born April 7, 1898, and died December 8, 1908. Fate was definitely in charge of her life that day.

One of five children of Mr. and Mrs. Logan Womack, Nannie and two of her brothers attended Mt. Olive School. Normally, these brothers would have been walking home with her that day, but as fate would have it, they had gone home with some friends that day. Even so, some friends walked home from school with Nannie until they reached the lane that branched off and led to Nannie's home. They asked if she wanted them to walk on home with her, but she said she was not afraid to walk alone. They waved good-bye, and she turned and walked down the lane alone. She was found murdered in that lane, less than a quarter mile from her home.

The woods that lined the lane were dark and thick and made a perfect hiding place for her killer, Elmer Hill. Elmer was a cousin of Nannie's, but he did not have a good reputation in the community. He was in his early twenties when he waited for Nannie to come by that day. He grabbed her, dragged her into the woods, and raped and murdered her. From bits of information pieced together later, Elmer was really waiting for one of the local girls and was upset when she didn't show up. Fate stepped in and sent him an innocent substitute—Nannie Womack.

Elmer attempted to murder Nannie with her scarf, but she survived his choking attempt. If only she had played dead, she might have lived. Perhaps she was too young to think of staying perfectly still. She was probably so frightened, she just wanted her mother.

As Elmer turned to walk away, Nannie sat up and called out three times, "Mama! Mama! Mama!"

It was then that Elmer turned back and smashed her small head and face with a tree limb. Strangely enough, at that same time, Nannie's mother, Jocie Hill Womack, thought she heard her daughter calling her. That was one of the reasons that made them start searching for her as soon as they did. (We talked recently to the man who moved not long ago with his family into a home near the place where Nannie was murdered. Some members of the family have heard the voice of a little girl calling, "Mama! Mama! Mama!")

The family was joined in the search by neighbors throughout the Webbs Cross Roads and Mt. Olive communities. Clay Dameron was the person who discovered Nannie's body.

While the search was on for the little girl, Elmer is said to have gone to the home of his grandfather to change clothes and hide his bloody ones in the loft. Later, he changed his shoes for a pair of new ones at the home of a man named Holt near the Blair Schoolhouse Road. Nobody ever explained why he went there to get the new shoes. Maybe blood was on the old pair.

In those days, it was the custom to "lay out" the body at home while the coffin was being built. During that time, Elmer came to the house to view his poor little dead cousin. He put on a good act. He was quoted as saying, "A person who would do a deal like that is sure a mean person!" At that point, nobody knew the mean person was Elmer himself.

Elmer joined the men outside who were discussing the crime and how to catch the killer. There was some mention of burning the killer at the stake when they caught him. A rider rode up and announced that bloodhounds were on their way from Lincoln County and would soon be there to start the search for the killer. This news seemed to upset Elmer, and he left the Womack home in a hurry. At that point, nobody had made the connection between Elmer and the murder.

The bloodhounds arrived and trailed the killer for three days before finding him in a relative's outbuilding in Sano, Kentucky, on the fourth day. Wolford Wilson and a young man named Sheperd captured Elmer among his relatives on Sunday, December 13, 1908, and took him to the Jamestown jail. Because of people's emotions running so high and the danger of lynching being very real, the authorities soon moved Elmer to the Wayne County jail, where he remained until Tuesday of the following week.

On the night of Elmer's arrest, a mob said to be composed of 25 to as many as 150 men decided to take the law into their own hands and hang Elmer Hill. Several such attempts were foiled, but finally a mob, many of whose members were prominent citizens, proceeded to Wayne County and seized Elmer Hill from the jail. The sheriff was not present at the time, and the deputy offered up the keys to the jail to the mob with no resistance.

Elmer Hill was taken back to Jamestown to a large black oak tree near a place called Gaddins Spring. He was seated on a horse that belonged to Nannie's grandfather. There, on the road coming up from Cumberland River, the men hanged Elmer Hill from the oak tree and left his body hanging there for all to see. Officials eventually came out and cut his body down. His unmarked grave is supposed to be in or near a Jamestown cemetery. Only a few know the actual spot.

Reports of Elmer's last words vary. Some say he told the mob to go ahead because he had it coming. Others suggested that the mob might have made up those words to justify what they did to him. Some say he said he had planned to do the same thing to three other girls and only regretted that he couldn't live long enough to do it. Guilty or innocent, he was deprived of a fair trial by the hanging.

There are reports of sightings of Elmer Hill's ghost in the

area where he was hanged. One child on his way to school reported seeing him hanging in the tree where he died. Two travelers who had a flat tire near where the lynching took place claim a man stood and watched them change the tire before disappearing. They described the man when they arrived at the place where they were staying for the night and learned that the ghostly watcher resembled Elmer Hill.

Considering that people still hear a little girl calling for her mama and see a restless figure appearing near the place of Elmer Hill's lynching, it seems that neither the victim nor the killer has yet found peace on the other side.

The Russellville Ghost

Stories of the ghost of a girl from Russellville is one of the most often told ghost stories in Kentucky. It is especially effective on stormy nights. We were so fascinated with the story that we went to Russellville a few summers ago to check it out. Unfortunately, the ghost did not make an appearance while we were there. Curious people like us still drive by to see if they can catch a glimpse of her.

Russellville is located in the southwest portion of Kentucky, just north of the Tennessee state line. The haunted house is located on Clarksville Road at a crossroads at a stoplight next to a cemetery.

This story has several variations, but the one most often told to us starts in a setting that is typical, yet perfect for ghost stories. This one truly started on a dark and stormy night!

On the night of this story, a young girl who lived in Russellville was dressed for a date that she had been looking forward to for a long time. Her parents had told her that she could go to a dance with her boyfriend if the weather was good. She spent the day in preparation for the big event. She was certain nothing would happen to spoil this evening for her.

As the afternoon wore on, however, dark clouds began to bank in the west. She began to feel uneasy as she heard a low rumble of thunder.

"Please don't let it storm tonight," she prayed silently, but her prayer went unanswered.

She looked out and saw that the clouds looked more threatening than ever. As night approached, so did the storm. She hoped the cloud would go in another direction, but it showed no indication of doing so.

The girl watched anxiously out the window for her date to arrive, but all she could see was the lightning, which flashed constantly and lit up the empty road. The storm hit at her house with violent winds and pouring rain. The girl was furious. It was so unfair! Her boyfriend was delayed because of the storm and didn't come. The wonderful evening she had planned was not going to happen. She stomped around the room, angry and frustrated. Her father tried to calm her down.

"You knew that we wouldn't let you go out in such a storm, even if the boy showed up," he said. "He was sensible to stay home. Travel on a night like this would be unsafe."

The girl didn't agree. She ran upstairs to her room. Still upset, she pressed her face against the window and stared once more into the storm. Angrily, she cursed God for letting the storm come and ruin her evening. Just then, a bolt of lightning struck. The charge ran through her body, killing her instantly. By some freak occurrence, a clear photographic imprint of her face was created in the pane of glass. Some believe that her curse caused her spirit to be trapped in the glass windowpane.

According to the story we heard, the parents wanted to keep the incident quiet to preserve their privacy, so they buried her in the cemetery close to their house. Soon after her burial, a strange thing began to happen. The dead girl's image was seen in the pane of glass on stormy nights! People began to come to the house to stare at the face in the window. Having people come and gawk at the house began to take its toll on the parents.

They tried to remove the face, but nothing they did would take the image away. They tried cleaning the glass and covering it with paint, but the face continued to appear. Eventually, they boarded up the window.

The girl's family no longer lives there, but it is still a private residence. The window is still boarded up, so nobody knows if the face still appears or not. When we were there, it was sunny and peaceful, so we did not bother the owners. The face only appears, it is said, on dark and stormy nights.

Odd Happenings at
Waverly Hills Sanatorium

We have been on many tours through Waverly, so we have personal experiences of our own to tell about. Many students in Roberta's classes at Pleasure Ridge Park High School sneaked into Waverly in the 1960s and 1970s because it was "the thing to do" to prove you were brave. These young people shared their experiences with us, too.

Waverly Hills Sanatorium, in southwestern Louisville, was formerly a tuberculosis hospital where thousands of people died before a cure was found for the deadly disease. Now it is famous for the ghosts of the dead who still linger there.

Tuberculosis was a disease that struck all ages. There were all types of people who were residents of the sanatorium, even entire families who became infected. Ghosts of children can be seen roaming the halls and playing in this now deserted place.

One night a tour guide was leading a group of tourists through Waverly when a question came up about the ghost of one of the children.

"I've heard there is a ghost of a little boy who plays with a blue ball here," a tourist said. "Is that true?"

"Yes," answered the guide. "We have reports of sightings of him. He was a patient here, but I haven't run into him myself."

The guide was taking a few steps backward as he answered the question, when he suddenly slipped and fell. The group looked down to see if he had been hurt by the fall. They were surprised by what they saw. There at his feet was a little blue rubber ball that had rolled from somewhere on its own.

"Well," said the guide, getting to his feet. "It looks like I've just had my first encounter!"

Other ghosts there seem to be indulging in their old habits. Some visitors see a tiny glowing ahead of them down the hall. One ghost sometimes comes out to meet the tour guests and have a smoke!

"When our smoker ghost was alive," said the guide, "she would often ask everybody she saw if they could spare a cigarette. You would think that someone suffering from a deadly lung disease would not be interested in smoking, but I guess she figured the damage had already been done."

Not all ghosts at Waverly are human, and not all groups who go there are led by tour guides. Before the current owners, Charles and Tina Mattingly, purchased the building and tightened security, it was like a "rite of passage" for boys to prove their courage by sneaking into the building and exploring alone. Some boys had heard that a homeless man and his dog had wandered into Waverly and died there. Their ghosts were said to roam the halls. The boys didn't know whether to believe the story or not, so they sneaked inside to try to find out for themselves. They were soon to wish that they had stayed outside.

They were about halfway down the hall when they heard a low growl of what sounded like a dog in the area where the old elevator shaft had been. It had been closed off after the homeless man and his dog had supposedly fallen to their death down the shaft. No electricity was on in the building, so the boys couldn't see the dog. Suddenly the empty elevator shaft lit up, and they heard the dog again. The growling seemed to be very near.

The boys ran as fast as they could, but the dog seemed to be gaining on them. They reached the outside door, thinking the dog was sure to leap at them. It did not follow them through the door, though. They fell to the ground to catch their breath, but all was silent behind them, like nothing had ever been there at all.

Steamboat Ghosts

We have heard steamboat stories from crew members and read them in articles we found online. We experienced some paranormal happenings ourselves.

Steamboats have a certain romantic, haunting appeal in our history. Though the Delta Queen *was not Louisville's own, Louisville citizens have always felt a special connection to this wonderful old boat because of the former annual steamboat races between the* Delta Queen *and the* Belle of Louisville.

The Great Steamboat Race was a yearly event that took place the Wednesday before the first Saturday in May, three days before the Kentucky Derby. It started in 1963 and continued each year through 2008. The race started underneath the George Rogers Clark Memorial Bridge, continued to Six Mile Island, and then returned to the bridge, covering a distance of fourteen miles. Other vessels joined the competition occasionally, but the races through the years were mainly between the Belle of Louisville *and the* Delta Queen. *They battled for the prize of the Golden Antlers, which passed fairly evenly back and forth between the two boats.*

People booked passage on the boats to take part in the race, and people lined the banks of the Ohio River every year until the Delta Queen *was retired as a competitor and turned into a dry-dock hotel in 2009. Some believed that, in addition to the usual live passengers on board, there was a ghostly passenger as well,* Delta Queen *captain Mary Green.*

Captain Mary Green was one of the nation's first female riverboat pilots. She died in her cabin on the *Delta Queen* in 1949. During her life on the *Delta Queen,* she did not believe in the sale of alcohol and refused to allow it to be served on the boat. After her death, a saloon was established on board. Immediately after the first drink was served, a barge bearing Captain Green's name rammed the *Delta Queen* and destroyed the bar. Was it coincidence? Maybe, but, if so, it was a very odd one.

There have been many sightings of Captain Mary on deck, but perhaps the most dramatic account that river lore gives us was told by retired captain Mike Williams. In 1984, Captain Williams was sleeping in his bunk on the *Delta Queen* when he woke up to a whisper in his ear. He could feel someone's breath, but there was no one there. He ignored it at first, but after it happened twice more, he got up to check. He found nobody there, but he did find water flowing into the lower level of the steamboat. A hole big enough to sink the boat was found and repaired. He believes that he was warned by the ghost of Captain Mary Green, a kind and watchful spirit that still lurks on deck looking out for her boat. If not for this warning, Captain Williams might not have awakened in time to find the hole and save the *Delta Queen* from sinking. It seems that Captain Mary stays on board to watch out for the welfare of the passengers.

The *Delta Queen* is now docked on the Tennessee River at Coolidge Park Landing in Chattanooga North Shores. On June 5, 2009, the renovated steamboat opened as the Delta Queen Hotel. It has the distinction of being the only floating Historic Hotel in America and is considered one of the most haunted ships in the United States. Guests still have occasional encounters with Captain Mary's friendly spirit.

Out of respect for this great steamboat, the Golden Antlers were retired when the *Delta Queen* retired. Now the winner of the annual race with the *Belle of Louisville* and its competitor receives Silver Antlers. Even though the *Delta Queen* no longer sails the waters of the Ohio River, the great old steamboat and the spirit of Captain Mary Green will live on forever in Louisville.

Stories from Homefolks

Stories from homefolks are the ones we like best. They take us back to times when we sat on the front porch in good weather, or inside by the fire when the weather was bad, and shared stories with family and friends. History is embedded in these tales, but mostly they reflect personal experiences told for entertainment. Most of the storytellers are long gone, but their stories live on.

Some stories from history are very similar to stories from homefolks. In some cases, we had a hard time deciding which story belonged in which category. The tales in this section are about people we knew, or they were told by someone who was close to the story itself. Some of them illustrate beliefs and customs in times past.

Medicine for Willie

Roberta's great-grandmother Alley was an "herb woman" who help treat the sick near her home in the Kentucky hills. She died before we were born, but her stories were passed on to her daughter, Lou Ann, who, in turn passed them to her son, Tom Simpson. We heard them from Tom and Lou Ann.

In the early 1900s in Kentucky, doctors used to stretch their services over large areas. Paying house calls meant they couldn't always be at a central location when they were needed. Women in the different neighborhoods who had knowledge of herbs and home remedies were often called on by their neighbors to help the sick and injured when a doctor was not immediately available.

Granny Burton was always called on to sit with the sick, especially children. Neighbors helped each other out like that back then because parents would often be completely worn out from trying to take care of a sick child day and night and then do their regular chores, too.

Granny was always more than happy to help when she was called on. She had learned quite a lot about herbs and healing from her mother. In fact, she planted an herb garden every year and tended it with loving care, so she would have the herbs she needed for remedies. Each year, she would harvest her crop and store everything carefully so she would always have a supply on hand.

She had to admit to herself that her favorite patient was Little Willie Dunbar, who lived on the next farm. Little Willie was a sickly boy who often caught colds that sent him to bed with a high fever. Granny Burton spent many nights through Little Willie's childhood, doctoring him with a poultice or herbs to heal a sore or break a fever. Regardless of how bad Little Willie felt, he always had a smile for everybody and tried not to be any trouble. Granny Burton would keep the fire going in the fireplace, keep Little Willie covered with Mrs. Dunbar's handmade quilts, and let Mr. and Mrs. Dunbar get some sleep.

"You always take better care of me than anybody," Little Willie told Granny Burton. "Promise you'll always come when I'm sick."

"Well, of course, I promise," said Granny Burton.

Unfortunately, Granny Burton was a little hasty with her promise. Suddenly one day, without any warning, Granny Burton died of a heart attack. Everybody was deeply shocked because nobody had known she had a heart problem. She had never complained, so maybe she herself didn't know how serious her condition was. Nobody was around to take her place nursing the sick. The Dunbar family especially missed her.

Little Willie insisted on going to Granny Burton's funeral with his parents. It was a chilly day and his parents didn't want to take him out, but he was so persistent in his intent to go that they finally gave in. As Little Willie stood by Granny Burton's grave, he realized he should have listened to his parents. He could feel the damp air sinking into his bones, and by the time the funeral ended and he got home, he was chilling and running a fever. The local doctor came and left some medicine, but he had to be on his way to pay another house call.

Mrs. Dunbar was afraid that Willie's chill might turn into pneumonia, so she bundled the little boy up in the quilts she had made for him. She sat by the fire to make sure he didn't kick the covers off. He was due to be given another dose of medicine in two hours, and she wanted to be sure to stay awake to give it to him.

Little Willie slept fitfully at first, but he finally settled into a peaceful sleep. His mother, tired from the household chores and from Granny Burton's funeral, sat in her rocking chair in front of the warm fire. The flames danced in the fireplace, and the penetrating heat relaxed her exhausted body. Soon she was fast asleep. Time passed, but she was not aware of it.

Then suddenly, she woke up. She wasn't sure what woke her, but she saw that dawn was breaking. Her first thought was that she had missed giving Little Willie his medicine and had let the fire go out. She could see that the fire was burning, though, and the room was warm. She stood up and moved quickly from her chair to Little Willie's bed. She was sure he would be feeling worse without his medicine, but he opened his eyes and smiled up at her.

"Honey, I am so sorry," she said. "I fell asleep and didn't give you your medicine. I'll get it for you right now."

"Wait, Momma!" he said. "I've already had my medicine."

"Son, I've told you not to get out of bed and get medicine

by yourself," she scolded gently. "Why didn't you wake me up?"

"I didn't get up, and I didn't need to wake you," he told her.

"Then how did you get your medicine?" she asked him.

"Granny Burton brought it to me," he told her.

"That's impossible!" exclaimed Mrs. Dunbar. "You must have been out of your head with fever! Granny Burton is dead!"

"I know she's dead, Momma," said Little Willie, "but I woke up and she was right here by my bed. She put her finger to her lips and shook her head so I'd be quiet and not wake you. Then she brought me my medicine and tucked the quilts around me. After that, she put some wood in the fireplace, and just vanished."

"That just couldn't happen, honey," she told Little Willie. "Are you sure you weren't dreaming?"

"I'm sure," he insisted. "She opened the bottle and gave my medicine to me."

Mrs. Dunbar looked at the bottle on the dresser. She could see that the level of liquid was down in the bottle and the spoon beside the bottle had traces of medicine on it. The bottle and spoon definitely had been used.

Mrs. Dunbar couldn't understand it. She asked her husband if he got up and gave Little Willie his medicine, but he insisted that he had slept through the night. Little Willie never changed his story. He knew Granny Burton had kept her promise, even though he didn't know how she could have done it.

After a while, Mrs. Dunbar began to believe the story. There was no other explanation for what had happened. At other times after that when Little Willie got sick, she would notice small signs that Granny Burton had paid a ghostly visit to watch over Little Willie. She would just smile and say a silent thank you to Granny Burton for taking care of her child while she got a good night's sleep.

Ghosts in the Graveyard

Tom Simpson told us this story. We thought of Tom and Edgar as the Tom Sawyer and Huckleberry Finn of their day.

Country living did not always offer a lot of excitement for growing boys in the early 1900s, so they often manufactured their own. Sometimes they got more excitement than they could handle.

Two young friends, Tom and Edgar, had heard graveyard tales all their lives while sitting around listening to older folks weave their magic with words. One of their favorite graveyard stories was told in different versions as part of many cultures. A neighbor said it really happened to his aunt in Kentucky. Edgar had read that it happened to a man named Ivan in Russia. Tom once met a man from South America who told him it happened to a child in that country.

The story has a simple plot. A person (man, woman, or child) is told that there is an odd grave in the local cemetery where a strange woman was buried long ago. This spirit did not like to be bothered, and she would reach up from the grave and grab anyone who dared to come to her grave and disturb her in any way. She would pull the person down into the grave, and the visitor would be lost forever. After hearing the story, the listener is challenged to go alone to the grave one night and stick some object (a knife, machete, fork, or whatever is appropriate in that culture) into the grave to prove his or her courage. The person making the challenge would tell the listener that he, the teller of the tale, would go in the morning to retrieve the object from the grave and return it to the brave owner.

In the story, the person goes to the grave and kneels to stick whatever he has brought into the grave. The poor person, being so frightened, doesn't realize that the object has pierced through a garment (a cape, jacket, raincoat, or whatever), thus pinning the visitor to the grave. When the person tries to stand up and realizes that something is holding him, he assumes it is the ghost's hand reaching up from the grave and grabbing him, so he dies of fright. The challenger goes to the grave the next morning and is shocked to find the person's body across the grave.

Tom and Edgar didn't believe anything drastic would happen to anyone who stuck something in a grave, but they did believe it would be a perfect prank to play on their not-so-brave friend Clarence. The more they thought about it, the more they knew they had to do it. It would be so funny to hide and watch Clarence approach the grave.

First, they found an old grave at the back of the cemetery by an old community church. Then they told Clarence the story, showed him the grave in daylight, and dared him to go alone at night and stick his new pocketknife in it.

Clarence resisted at first, but he finally agreed to do it just to shut them up.

"You guys have got to come along and stay close by," he told them.

They considered it and decided it might be fun to go along as far as the cemetery gate and watch, but they had to agree to come running if Clarence called for help.

They picked a late summer night when a steady rain was falling to put their prank in motion. They made a point of wearing their lightweight raincoats in the hope that Clarence would stick his knife through his coat and freak out.

As they approached the cemetery, rumbles of thunder and jagged streaks of lightning in the distance provided the perfect atmosphere. Their nerves were a bit unsteady as they opened the gate and silently pointed Clarence toward the grave in the old section in the back. Clarence took a few steps and stopped, losing his nerve altogether.

"I don't think this is such a good idea," he said. "It's disrespectful. Nothing good can ever come from disturbing the dead."

Tom and Edgar looked at each other. Their prank was not going as planned.

"Nothing's going to happen, Clarence," Edgar assured him. "It's not like we're digging her up or anything."

"You're just scared," said Tom. "I knew you'd chicken out. Come on. Let's all go stick our pocketknives in the grave."

The idea of not being alone boosted Clarence's courage. "Okay," he said. "Let's go."

Tom and Edgar took the lead, and Clarence followed closely behind. It didn't take long until they had crossed the cemetery and reached the grave they had chosen. Knives in hand, they raised their arms to plunge the blades into the earth, when suddenly a bolt of lightning danced on the old tombstone and thunder crashed angrily overhead. The rain turned to a white mist that rose from the grave and engulfed the boys. They felt an intense, unearthly cold penetrating their raincoats. Even though it was summer, they felt a sudden chill as they had never felt before. Shivering and without saying a word, they turned in unison and ran for the gate.

Tom and Edgar were in the lead again, with Clarence not far behind, trying with all his might to keep up. Suddenly, he stumbled and grabbed a tall tombstone to break his fall.

"Wait!" he screamed to Tom and Edgar. "It's on my back! Get it off! Get it off!"

Tom and Edgar stopped and looked back through the light mist that was still clinging to them. They could barely see Clarence, but they could tell that he was struggling with something.

"Hold on, Clarence! We're coming!" they yelled in the same breath.

They reached the obviously terrified Clarence, who was now gasping for air. They realized the best way to help him was to get him out of there as fast as they could. Each grabbed an arm and literally dragged Clarence along between them. They couldn't see anything on his back, but both boys felt that he weighed as much as two people!

The rain let up as they reached the gate, and the mist dissolved as they pulled Clarence through. Once outside the cemetery, the stricken boy's breathing returned to normal, and he was able to stand and move on his own. The three ran from the graveyard as fast as they could. They never went back there again at night. Later, when they looked at the graveyard through the church windows on Sunday mornings, they could still feel the penetrating cold.

From that night on, Tom and Edgar sat in storytelling circles and heard that old tale told and retold. They no longer thought it was just a harmless story. They vowed never to play a prank like that again. They had come to believe that Clarence was right. Nothing good could ever come from disturbing the dead!

Under the Bed

There was a peculiar old custom in Kentucky of putting a birthday person under the bed on his or her birthday. The more times the person was put under the bed, the more he or she was loved and the more good luck would come to the birthday person the following year. Some people believed that this practice should stop at the child's ninth birthday because bad luck would come after that. It was said that the child would never grow after the age of nine if the custom continued past that year, but no reason was given for why this particular age was the cut-off point or what might cause the bad luck from then on.

This practice is mostly forgotten now, but it persisted into the middle 1900s. In fact, each of us experienced it, but we never heard where it came from.

The custom of putting the birthday person under the bed spoiled all the fun for Coy Norcliff on his birthday each year. He couldn't remember the year he was put under the bed for the first time. The years ran together in his mind; but from years in his former home, he could remember dust bunnies and a slight feeling of claustrophobia. He hadn't enjoyed these experiences, but he hadn't been terrified either. He only felt uncomfortable then. The terror had come in this house last year for the first time, and he hadn't been able to forget it.

His relatives had come for dinner, and they had brought presents. They all had an enjoyable time until the celebration was almost over. He was taken completely by surprise when his two older cousins grabbed him. His parents and his aunt and uncle had watched and laughed as they pulled him to the floor and pushed him under the bed. Coy had struggled violently and finally managed to shove his cousins away and escape by crawling out the other side. He was pale, shaking, and gasping for air when he emerged.

"Don't you ever do that to me again," he said to his cousins, his voice quivering with rage.

Everybody was surprised at his reaction.

"It was just a joke, Coy," his mom said. "Why are you so upset?"

"There is something under there," he told her. "It's something awful."

His cousins didn't believe he could possibly be serious. They began to laugh and tease him.

"A monster!" said one cousin.

"A ghost?" asked the other.

Coy didn't bother to answer them. He knew no one would believe him. He said as little as possible until his relatives left. Then, when his parents asked, he told them what had happened.

Coy had never talked about it before, but he had seen signs of the ghost from the first day he and his family moved into this farmhouse. It began with a tapping on the floor under his bed as soon as he lay down at night. After he managed to get to sleep, he would wake to soft moaning sounds and the covers being pulled off his bed. Once he heard a noise on the floor beside his bed and rolled to the edge to see what it was. He glanced down and saw something on the floor, but it was gone in an instant. He was too frightened to remember many details, but it looked like a girl with long, stringy hair.

Today, when his cousins had pushed him under the bed, he had seen the thing clearly. The pale, ghostly face with rotting teeth and long, stringy hair was right there, inches from his face. It was reaching for him as he pushed his way out from under the bed. It was trying to take his breath away!

Coy was relieved at first to be telling his parents about his experiences, but by the time he finished, he could tell they didn't believe him. His mom explained that all old houses have noises of their own, and his dad mumbled something about how he would eventually get adjusted to his surroundings and not be frightened at night.

"There is a logical reason for everything," his mom told him, and his father agreed.

If they thought they were comforting him, they were wrong. Coy disregarded everything they said. There were no logical reasons for the things that were happening in his room. Something was definitely under his bed, and he did not want to join it on his ninth birthday next year. He remembered that he shouldn't have to worry, though. This silly custom was supposed to stop at age nine.

The next year passed quickly. Coy knew the thing was still under the bed, but he felt like it would stay there and not bother him if he did not bother it. He said nothing else about it to his parents.

As his ninth birthday approached, Coy managed to convince himself that nobody would put him under the bed this year. His relatives were coming again this year, but he thought he'd gotten his point across to his cousins last year. He thought they'd leave him alone.

Finally his birthday came. His uncle, aunt, and two cousins came over to celebrate again. He and his cousins played outside until it was time to eat. After they'd had their fill of cake and homemade ice cream, Coy opened his presents. Nobody mentioned the incident of the previous year, so Coy was relaxed by the time he opened his last gift.

Then it happened. His cousins grabbed him from behind, dragged him to his bed, and stuffed him under. Initially, he started to struggle, but then, his cousins said later, he just went limp. Frightened, they pulled him out, but he was barely breathing. The family rushed him to the doctor.

Doc Evans had just returned to his office from making a house call in the country when they brought Coy in. His family stayed in the waiting room while Doc Evans did the examination. Doc's wife brought them some coffee.

"Did you folks know about the people who lived in your house before you moved in?" she asked.

They all shook their heads.

"It was a sad situation," she continued. "The couple had a daughter that was born not quite right in the head. She couldn't talk, so they made her sleep on a pallet by their bed. She'd moan or pull the covers off if she needed something. One night, she just up and died. Her heart just stopped. She was only nine years old."

She finished her story just as Doc Evans came into the room. His somber look told the family the bad news, even before he spoke.

"I'm so sorry," he told them. "I couldn't save him. He had a severe shock and his heart simply stopped."

Did Coy actually see a ghost under the bed that took his breath away? Was it the girl who died in the house before him? Were people right about children not growing if they were put under the bed on their ninth birthday?

The Norcliff family would never have those answers for sure, but one thing was certain. Coy didn't need to grow past his ninth birthday to fit into his small homemade coffin.

The Woman Who Was Almost a Ghost

Several years ago, the Louisville Ghost Hunters held the Mid-South Paranormal Conference at Waverly Hills Sanatorium. An area was set aside for book signings and paranormal readings. Many people walked by our table, but the crowd often came in spurts. One afternoon when the crowd had thinned out, a man walked up to our table and asked if we had a minute. Of course, we said yes. He said he would rather not give his name because he thought there might be people connected to his story who might still be living, and he didn't have their permission to tell the story. He said that he needed to tell someone, though; the story bothered him because it was so strange.

When he mentioned the name of the house, we recognized it immediately. We had passed it on a tour organized by Robert Parker, Mr. Ghost Walker. We had heard lots of strange stories about the house, but we had never heard this one. If you are interested in taking the tour, contact Mr. Ghost Walker (502-689-5117).

There is an old house in Louisville that was once used as a family dwelling, with one section used as an office by a doctor in family. It was rumored that this doctor used to perform illegal abortions in this office, but it was a subject mostly kept hush-hush.

Many years passed and the family moved away. The

doctor closed his practice and died a few years later. The rumors died with him, and the house stood empty.

One day, a man and his wife were walking down the street where the old house stood. As they approached, the woman stopped abruptly and held tightly to her husband's arm. She had never seen the house before, but she became very fearful and began to shake.

"What's wrong?" asked her husband.

"I don't know," she said. "It's that house! I can't go near it!"

"We'll be by it soon," he said. "There's nothing there to hurt you."

He urged her on, but still she clung tightly to her husband. By the time they were even with the doctor's old office, the woman began to cry and tremble uncontrollably. She had never acted this way before, and her behavior surprised both her and her husband. He was at a total loss as to what he should do, so he practically pulled her down the street. When they got past the house, she calmed down and felt normal again. Neither could figure out why she acted so strangely.

After they arrived home, the woman's two uncles happened to come by for a visit. She was always glad to see them because the rest of her family was dead. She had always felt particularly close to these uncles.

"You look a little pale," one uncle said. "Are you feeling okay?"

"Yeah," agreed the other uncle. "You look like you've seen a ghost!"

Still a little shaky from the odd experience at the old house, she told them what had happened. Her husband confirmed the strange incident.

The uncles listened without interrupting. When she finished, they exchanged glances. Then one uncle spoke.

"I guess there is something you should know," he said. "It might explain what happened."

"Then tell me, please," she said.

"The family never wanted you to know," he said, "but when your mother was carrying you, she was having a very difficult time. Finally, it got too much for her, so she went to the doctor at that house to get an abortion. The two of us were at the house when she left, and we followed her to see where she was going. No one in our family supported abortion, so we rushed into the doctor's office just as he was ready to abort you! We stopped him and took your mother home. Your mother always regretted what she almost did and was grateful to us for stopping her from making a terrible mistake. Maybe that accounts for the way you felt."

The woman and her husband thought about it and decided that maybe that was the explanation. Maybe somehow she had slipped back in time and felt what she may have felt in the womb when she almost became a ghost before she was born!

The Bathtub Ghost

We lived down the road from the Wilsons, so we heard Mr. Wilson tell this story often. We have retold it here in our own words.

Indoor plumbing was not a typical luxury for people in our neighborhood. We were excited to have an inside bathroom, and we never took our good fortune for granted.

Olivia and Luther Wilson lived on a small farm for many years without any modern conveniences like indoor plumbing. As they got older, they found it more difficult to take sponge baths in wash pans and to go to the outhouse. After he had an especially profitable year from his crops, Luther had inside plumbing installed and put in a bathtub for his "Livie," as he called Olivia.

Livie had a touch of arthritis, and it eased her aching joints to sit in a hot bath. Luther warned her to be careful because the tub was slick. He tried to arrange to be inside when she got into the tub as a small measure of safety. That worked well in the winter, but when spring came Luther had to be outside most of the day planting crops.

One morning, Livie's joints were particularly achy, so she ran herself a hot bath while Luther was plowing the fields. She added some lilac-scented bath oil that she always loved to use and then eased herself into the water and relaxed. She rubbed her bar of soap up and down her arms and over her face. The soap bubbles got in her eyes and began to burn. She grabbed a towel and didn't notice that the bar of soap had slid down into the bath water.

As the burning in her eyes ceased, Livie decided to get out of the tub and dry off. As she stood up, her foot hit the bar of soap and she slipped and fell, knocking herself unconscious on the edge of the tub.

It was close to lunchtime when her accident happened, so it wasn't long until Luther came in from the fields to eat and found her. He quickly lifted her from the water and summoned help, but Livie never regained consciousness.

Luther couldn't believe what had happened. He was lost without his Livie. The work in the fields was all that kept him sane. He talked about her to anyone who would listen.

He blamed himself for her death. If he hadn't bought that bathtub, she'd still be alive. It was his fault that she was gone from him forever.

He had never thought much about the afterlife. He had left that kind of thing to Livie. Now he didn't know what to think. He just knew he needed her and she was no longer there.

And then something happened that made him think that our loved ones never leave us—that they are near after death and come to us when we need them most.

It was a bright summer Sunday morning. Luther was getting ready to walk the half-mile to the little country church as he and Livie had done while they had been married. His work in the fields had left him all dirty and sweaty and, even though he had washed up, he still felt the need for a hot bath.

He hated getting in the tub now. Every time he did, he saw Livie there in his mind, unconscious and helpless. Today, he didn't have time to dawdle, though. Time was slipping away, and he didn't want to be late for church.

He ran the water until it was hot and the tub was about half full. Then he carefully eased himself down into the water, ever mindful now of how easy it was to slip. The water felt good and he felt relaxed and sleepy. He was almost dozing off when he heard the clock in the hall start striking. He had to hurry if he was to get to church on time.

He rose quickly and stood straight in the tub. Then suddenly, everything started to go around and around! He had gotten up too fast and now he was dizzy. He reached for something to hold onto, but he felt himself tilting backward. He couldn't find anything to hold onto. He was going to fall in that tub just like Livie!

But then, two hands steadied him. His head stopped spinning, and he regained his balance. He was able to step safely out of the tub. As he dried off, he smelled the scent of lilacs that Livie always used. He knew he certainly had not put any scented bath oil into his bath. He could hardly believe it, but he knew Livie had saved him.

He smiled as he walked to church that morning. Maybe other people would not be able to see why he was so happy, but he knew Livie was there walking beside him.

The Ghost Who Disturbed Children

This story came directly from Lonnie's youngest sister, Wanda. Both she and her sister do not scare easily. Whatever happened had to be very strange indeed to make them nervous or frightened.

Many years ago, Wanda moved with her husband, children, and parakeet to an old house in Louisville. It had several eerie features that spooked her right from the first. Not long after they moved in, she set about cleaning the basement and found some old bones on a shelf under the window. They looked like they might be the bones of rats or birds, but she never learned for sure what kind of bones they were or how they got there. Regardless of what they were, she didn't want them occupying any part of her basement, so she threw them in the garbage.

She heard that the house had once been a doctor's office. She wondered if he might have used the bones some way in his practice. She couldn't imagine how, though.

There was one other thing about the house that really bothered her. Whenever she went to the basement, she felt she was being watched. Her washer was in the basement, so she had no choice about going down there. She would stuff her clothes in the washing machine and run back upstairs. Sometimes, the presence she felt would be so strong and unpleasant that she would leave her clothes in the washer for quite a while until she got up enough courage to go down and take them out. The good thing was that the presence never came upstairs—until one disturbing night.

Wanda's husband worked at night, so Wanda was glad when her oldest sister, Nellie, and her children came up from the country to visit. The cousins were especially happy to be together.

The evening passed quietly and bedtime approached. Wanda and Nellie got the beds made up for the children and themselves. Wanda put the cover over her parakeet's cage, and they all settled down to sleep.

Suddenly, the parakeet started a ruckus like they had never heard. It squawked loudly and flew wildly around its cage. Wanda took the cover off to see what was causing it to act that way, but she saw nothing there except a very frightened bird. She was puzzled because the bird usually went right off to sleep when she covered the cage. She waited a few minutes while it still carried on, but she finally gave up waiting for it to settle down completely. She covered the cage and went back to bed. Once again, they all tried to sleep.

Sleep did not come easy. As they were drifting off, a thud pulled them back into reality. They were surprised to see that one of the children had fallen out of the bed. They got up and checked the child; fortunately, she wasn't hurt. They all went back to bed, and just as they were relaxing, they heard another thud. Another child had rolled out of bed.

For the rest of the night, the bird fussed and the children fell out of bed, one by one. They were not hurt, but they were really scared. They weren't playing a joke. They were tired and sleepy, and getting a little cranky because they wanted to sleep. Something was determined, however, that none of the family would sleep that night. Finally, around 4:00 a.m., the activity stopped. The bird got quiet, and the rest of the night passed without incident.

Wanda never could figure out why the ghost picked the children to disturb that night. Even though nothing else happened while they lived there, Wanda and her husband found another house as soon as they could and moved away.

The Dove

This story came from one of Lonnie's uncles. It was often repeated in storytelling sessions.

Early settlers and those who lived in rural areas through World War II were accustomed to having guns in their homes. Rifles (known as the twenty-two) were useful in hunting rabbits, squirrels, and certain birds for food. Many boys had a rifle of their own by the time they were eleven or twelve years old. They hunted with their fathers and would use tin cans as target practice when left alone to provide their own entertainment.

Hunters were legally permitted to shoot turkeys, quail, pheasant, geese, and ducks for food, and they were allowed to shoot hawks that attempted to carry off their chickens. Some birds were not to be killed, though.

The dove was one bird they did not shoot. Many believed it to be a sacred bird. Children were told the story of the dove bringing an olive branch to Noah on the ark to show that the danger from the flood was gone. The dove became a Christian symbol of the Holy Spirit and the international sign for peace. Some Native Americans believed it was bad luck to kill a dove because it was believed to contain the soul of a lover. Some people also believed that the dove was sacred because it was the one bird into which witches and even the Devil could not transform.

Twelve-year-old Eugene Long had heard these beliefs for as long as he could remember. He had just received a twenty-two rifle for his birthday, so he was not surprised when his mom and dad reminded him of all these things. They stressed that he must never kill a mockingbird, a dove, or a songbird of any kind. Eugene assured them that he would not do that, so they allowed him to go out alone with his new rifle.

It was late afternoon the day before Thanksgiving, and it was Eugene's plan to kill a turkey all by himself for Thanksgiving dinner. Yesterday, he and his dad had spotted some turkeys down by the creek in the edge of the woods in back of the field behind the barn. Eugene was very excited as he walked past the barn and his mother's chicken coops.

He could hardly wait to surprise his whole family by bringing home a turkey all by himself. The idea made him feel very grown up and important.

He approached the creek and wooded area very quietly. His eyes searched along the creek bank as he waited for the turkeys to appear. The minutes crawled by without any sign of the turkeys, but Eugene was patient. The sun dropped out of sight behind a dark bank of clouds in the west, and a cold wind picked up and made Eugene shiver. The clouds moved closer as he waited, and the air felt damp.

"It feels like snow!" Eugene said to himself.

The shadows deepened and began to close in, and Eugene had to admit that no turkeys were going to show up today at this location. He thought maybe he could go out again early Thanksgiving morning and try again. Disappointed, he started through the field toward the barn. With his hunt over for the day, he was now looking forward to the warm house and the delicious dinner his mother would soon have ready.

As he walked along, Eugene saw a bird land on top of the barn. It had appeared in a flash and he couldn't see it clearly, but the sound of startled chickens in the coops convinced him it was a hawk. His instinct was to protect his mother's chickens, so he stopped and took action without thinking. He placed the barrel of the rifle on the fence post to steady it, took quick aim, and pulled the trigger. His aim was perfect. The bird toppled from its perch and slid down the roof of the barn to the ground. Excited by the thought that he had killed a hawk, he ran to the bird and stopped abruptly when he saw his mistake. It wasn't a hawk at all. It was a dove, bleeding and dead, on the ground before him.

Eugene was stunned. How could this have happened? He had never meant to shoot a dove! He should have taken a closer look before shooting, but he was so thrilled at the chance to use his new rifle that he had neglected to do so. What was done was done, though. He couldn't change it. He knew he would be in trouble with his parents, but it was better to take the dove to the house and tell them what he had done than to leave it here and let them discover it. He picked the dove up and saw drops of its blood where it had landed on the ground. Guilt-stricken, he carried the bird home and showed his parents.

Their reaction was not as bad as he expected. Of course, they were unhappy about what he had done, but they could see that Eugene was truly sorry. They helped him bury the dove and then said no more about it.

Eugene had trouble sleeping that night. The clouds had moved in, and the wind howled and whistled and kept him awake until almost dawn. When he woke the next morning, there were three inches of freshly fallen snow on the ground.

While his mom cooked breakfast, Eugene went to the barn with his father to feed and milk the cows. As they approached, they noticed something unusual in the snow. They walked closer to examine it. There in the deep snow was a circle about the size of a large lard can lid. The ground inside the circle was in plain view. Not one flake of that three-inch snow was inside that circle.

"Dad," Eugene said in a hushed voice, "that is the spot where the dove fell after I shot it."

It was a long time before Eugene took his rifle out again, and he always made sure he knew his target before he fired.

Eugene had good reason to think of the dove during the rest of his years on the farm. When the winter snows came, the circle where the dove fell remained completely clear. When the green grass of spring and summer grew, it surrounded the circle of brown earth, but nothing ever grew in that circle.

People wondered if the spirit of the dove lived on after the bird's untimely death on the eve of Thanksgiving all those years ago.

Shadow of a Boy

This story came from Roberta's side of the family. Barbara Jane Alley told this to her sister Lou Ann, Roberta's grandmother, and Lou Ann passed it on.

When Barbara Jane was in her teens, she once spent a winter with relatives in southern Kentucky near the Tennessee state line. Her Uncle Samuel had broken his leg in a fall from a horse and was left weak and sick. He and Aunt Lou had two small girls, but they were too young to be of much help to their mother. Lou and Samuel had lost an older boy in an accident the winter before, so they needed a pair of strong, young hands to help out. Barbara Jane was used to hard work at home, and she was happy to stay with them when they asked her. Her presence was very welcome that winter.

Barbara Jane helped with the milking, cooking, cleaning, washing, and ironing. Aunt Lou often sent her through the woods close to their house to the country store to get whatever supplies the family needed. Barbara Jane enjoyed the walk, except for one spot. The path was narrow there and wound around rocks and stumps where sinister-looking shadows lurked. At this spot, the earth dropped sharply to a stream that flowed far below. Barbara Jane could see how easy it would be to lose her footing and plunge into the stream. It was the scariest part of the walk, so she made a point of being very careful there. She tried to avoid going into the woods at all after dark unless there was something the family absolutely had to have. She wasn't terribly frightened in the woods, but she had to admit to herself that the shadows spooked her a little when they looked so lifelike.

One day when she and Aunt Lou were preparing supper, Barbara Jean said, "Do you ever see people shadows in the woods when you walk there?"

"I haven't walked there in a long time, child," her aunt answered. " I don't pay much attention to such things. I guess there are lots of animals in there that might make shadows."

"I don't think what I see are animal shadows," said Barbara Jane. "Sometimes I think a shadow is following me, and it scares me a little. Do you avoid walking in the woods now because of shadows?"

"It's not shadows that keep me out," replied Aunt Lou. "It's memories of better times there."

Barbara Jane remembered that Uncle Samuel had fallen off his horse in the woods. She figured that that was what Aunt Lou was talking about, so she let the subject drop.

Barbara Jane continued to make trips through the woods to the store, and she often caught a glimpse of a shadow that seemed to be following her. She said nothing about it to her aunt and uncle. They often looked sad because it would soon be a year since their son had died. The fatal accident had happened at Christmastime, and the approaching Christmas season made them remember.

As Christmas grew near, Aunt Lou began making her annual Christmas goodies for the family and neighbors. She needed extra flour, lard, sugar, and spices for baking cookies, cakes, and pies and for making candy. This meant more frequent trips to the store by Barbara Jane.

On Christmas Eve, the house was full of wonderful smells, and the family ate heartily from the platter of ham, bowls of steaming vegetables, and special desserts. The family felt particularly blessed because Samuel was beginning to get his strength back. The two little girls were excited about Santa Claus coming, so it was hard to get them to bed. Finally, they wore themselves out and went to sleep.

"Barbara Jane," announced Aunt Lou, "it's time to get the presents we ordered for the girls."

"Where are they?" inquired Barbara Jane, looking toward the closet and then the attic door. "I'll help you fill their stockings and put their presents under the tree."

"Why, they're at the store, hon," said Aunt Lou. "Didn't I tell you? We always leave the presents at Harmon's store until Christmas."

"Why on earth do you do that?" asked Barbara Jane.

"Most folks around here do that," explained Aunt Lou. "There's no place to hide them at home. The Harmons don't mind keeping them so the little folks won't find them before Christmas. They live beside their store and it gives them a chance to visit with their neighbors on Christmas Eve when they come to pick up their purchases. Sometimes, it means an extra sale or two if people need something at the last minute. I filled the lantern for you. All you have to do is run there and back. It won't take long."

Barbara Jane felt her heart sink. Uncle Samuel had mentioned at supper that he heard on the radio that snow was coming in. She had not expected to be out tonight, but she couldn't let her little cousins down.

She put on her coat, scarf, and boots and lit the lantern Aunt Lou had filled for her. As soon as she stepped outside and started across the yard to the path in the woods, she knew she had more to worry about than the shadows tonight. Heavy snow had started to fall, and it was already sticking to the ground.

She ducked her head and crossed through the swirling snow to the path that led her into the woods. She hurried as fast as she could, but walking into the wind was hard. She knew the path would be completely covered on her return trip, so she tried to memorize other things by the path to mark her way home.

It took longer than usual, but she finally arrived at the store. Several others were there picking up their presents. The Harmons offered her some hot chocolate, but she didn't stay to visit. She took the huge bag of gifts and headed back out into the snow.

The voices from the store faded behind her as she moved deeper into the woods. Everything became silent as the snow blanketed the trees and ground, turning them into unfamiliar sleeping things. With the path snow-covered, Barbara Jane had trouble finding her way. She held up her lantern, but all it showed was snow in every direction. Everything was still and white like a forest morgue. She figured she must be nearing the drop-off above the stream, but nothing she saw confirmed that. She stopped and stood, frightened, trying to get her bearings.

"Nobody would find me if I fell into that stream to-night," she said aloud. "I would die for sure."

Her eyes filled with tears, but she realized she would freeze if she stayed still. She forced herself to move on, carefully taking one step at a time. Suddenly her foot hit something, and she slid to the right. She gasped as her body bumped into something that stopped her. She thought it must be the big rock near the drop, but it was snow-covered like everything else.

Then in the lantern light, a shadow flickered for an instant. She could feel something on the path in front of her, but she couldn't see it in the darkness. A calmness began to take over her whole being. She heard nothing, but she knew she should follow whatever was in front of her. She clutched the gifts and the lantern and stumbled along. She was lost, yet she felt something was leading her in the right direction. She walked and walked, and then she felt she was alone again. Whatever had led her was gone.

She looked around and saw that it was all right. She was at the edge of the woods, and she could see the light from the house in the window. She hurried with renewed energy and quickly reached the door.

Aunt Lou heard her footsteps and flung the door open.

"Oh, thank goodness you're safe!" she said, taking the lantern and gifts and helping Barbara Jane inside. "I didn't realize it was snowing like that when I sent you out. Did you have trouble finding the way?"

"Yes, it was awful," said Barbara Jane. "But you will never believe what happened."

As they stuffed stockings and wrapped the gifts and put them under the tree, Barbara Jane related the events of the evening to her uncle and aunt.

"A shadow led me home," said Barbara Jane. "I felt it keeping me safe."

"It was a miracle!" said Aunt Lou. "Did you know our boy died in the woods last year? He always went out on Christmas Eve to get the presents. It was one of his favorite things to do. Last year, he slipped over the drop and was killed in the fall. I've always heard that on Christmas Eve, the dead can leave their graves and walk the earth. Tonight, I think he came back to walk with you."

The Ghost Rider

Lillian Dean Simpson, Roberta's mother, told this story. It happened to her.

In the early 1900s, the flu swept through Kentucky. It showed no mercy and often left several members of the same family dead at the same time. In those days the flu was a new enemy, and nobody knew how to fight it. To make matters worse, there was a shortage of doctors. Each doctor had to cover a large territory because there were no hospitals to contain the infected patients in one place. Even when the doctor came, he had no medicine to wipe out this deadly disease.

In a society where neighbors were used to helping one another in time of sickness, the flu put an end to that custom. In some homes, every family member was sick and unable to help each other, much less go to help a neighbor. The people not infected were afraid to expose themselves for fear of getting sick themselves. This wasn't a disease that would just make them uncomfortable; this was a disease that would take their lives.

One man, Mr. Otis, was an exception. He rode his horse every day to every house in the neighborhood, bringing much-needed supplies and medicine to sick families. He also brought news of the community that everyone wanted to hear. Otis had never been the best-liked man in the area, but now he was a godsend. His main fault was his love for a drink of whiskey, and some of the more religious citizens in the community didn't approve of drinking. Otis thought a drink of whiskey would keep the flu away, so he would always take a drink of whiskey as he rode up to each house.

Otis never actually went inside the houses he visited. Whoever was able would come to the door when they heard the sound of his horse. He would give them whatever he had for them that day and then ride on to the next house.

In the Dean household, little Lillian was the only one in her family who did not come down with the flu. Her mother died from it, but her father, brother, and two sisters were still alive and suffering. Lillian was only nine and scared, so she welcomed the sight of Otis riding up to the door. He brought her one bit of news that likely saved her stricken family from death. He told her that everybody who took the third dose of medicine that the doctor was giving had died! He told her that an herb woman he knew had been giving herbs to patients that had helped them recover.

"Could you bring me some?" Lillian asked.

"Don't worry," he told her. "I'll get some and bring them tomorrow. Everything will be all right."

Lillian noticed that Otis looked tired and was coughing as he rode away. She turned her attention back to her family, though. The decision she had to make was a difficult one for a child of nine, but she could see that the doctor's medicine was not working. She had given them two doses of the medicine already, and her family seemed to get weaker instead of stronger. She decided not to give them that third dose. Instead, she gave each one some hot soup and let them rest.

Early the next morning, Lillian heard a horse coming. She ran to the door just in time to see Otis ride up and drop a bag by her door. He waved and rode off without a word. She thought nothing of it because he always had lots of places to go.

She took the bag of herbs inside and boiled them into a tea. All day, she gave the tea to each member of her family. By late afternoon, she could see that they were gaining strength. The fever broke in each of them, and though they were still far from completely well, Lillian knew they were all going to make it.

She was starting to make more soup for supper when she heard the sound of a horse and buggy. It was the doctor coming to pay a call. He inquired about the family, and she told him they were better now.

"Otis brought me some herbs this morning," she said.

"This morning?" the doctor asked.

"Yes," she answered. "I've been making tea from the herbs all day."

"Honey," said the doctor, "you must be getting sick yourself and imagining things. Otis died last night! He came down with the flu, but he forced himself to keep going until he collapsed."

Lillian knew she wasn't sick and she wasn't imaging things. Otis might have been a ghost, but he had brought her the herbs like he said he would. Her family was alive and recovering to prove it!

The Chime Child's Warning

Christmas, not Halloween, used to be the traditional time for ghost stories. We loved hearing them from our aunts and uncles who came for the Christmas holidays. We would settle down by the fireplace to munch Christmas goodies and hear stories, including those about the chime child.

A chime child is a child born when the clock chimes at midnight on Christmas Eve. It is widely believed that children born at this time are said to have the special gift of seeing ghosts and talking with the dead.

Mary Sinclair was a chime child. She didn't tell many people about her special gift because the few people she did tell had laughed at her. Her favorite aunt, Aunt Martha, never laughed, though, when Mary told her about some of her experiences. She took Mary's stories very seriously.

Aunt Martha was the sister of Mary's mother. The two sisters had been very sad when their mother died, even though she had been suffering for several months. Mary was sad, too, when she attended her grandmother's funeral that day. Later that night, she was drifting off to sleep when she saw her grandmother appear at the foot of her bed. Mary noticed that the pain was gone from the old lady's face and she was smiling a radiant smile. After a few seconds she faded away, and Mary went off to sleep. Seeing her grandmother's ghost did not frighten Mary. It made her feel better to know that her grandmother was still around.

The next morning, Mary told her mother and Aunt Martha about the visit from her grandmother, but her mom told her it was just a dream. Aunt Martha believed her, though, and took it as a sign that her mother had returned to let them know she was happy now and at peace.

Not long after her grandmother's death, Mary had another ghostly visitor. This time it was her cousin Orville, Aunt Martha's son, who was far away fighting in World War I. Mary awoke in the middle of the night to see someone standing beside her bed. The room was unusually cold, and she shivered as she pulled the covers tighter around her. She recognized her cousin in his uniform, but he had a wound in his head. He didn't speak to her, but she felt he had died and was trying to get a message to Aunt Martha to let her know it was okay and that he loved her. He vanished then, and once he had left, the temperature in the room felt normal again.

The next morning, Mary told her parents and Aunt Martha what she had seen and felt. Her mom and dad dismissed it as a dream, but Aunt Martha knew it was a sign that her son had died in battle. News traveled slowly then, so it was a few weeks before Aunt Martha received the news confirming Orville's death. Mary's experience comforted Aunt Martha in her loss because it confirmed her belief in life after death.

The loss of her son took its toll on Aunt Martha, though. That autumn, when all the leaves died, Aunt Martha died, too. Mary was heartbroken. She came home from the funeral, ate an early supper, and went to bed right away. She was sure that Aunt Martha would pay her a visit that night, but nothing happened. Mary was disappointed because she had wanted to see her aunt again.

Autumn turned into a very cold winter, and Mary's thoughts turned to Christmas and her birthday. She was hoping for a white Christmas, and she was delighted when she looked out the window on Christmas Eve morning and saw that her wish had been granted. Huge snowflakes were falling fast and sticking to the ground. The snow would surely be around for Christmas morning and beyond. Mary's father had gone into town very early to pick up some gifts and groceries so he could get back home before the roads became impassable. Mary and her mother were home alone.

After breakfast, Mary went to play in her room. Suddenly, she knew she was not alone. She looked up and saw Aunt Martha's face outside, looking in the window. She was very agitated, and it was clear she was trying to tell Mary something. In Mary's mind, she heard Aunt Martha say, "Help Ralph now!" Then it looked like she just melted into the falling flakes of snow.

Mary felt her sense of urgency. Her cousin Ralph was Aunt Martha's youngest son. He had been living alone on the farm next door after Aunt Martha had died. Aunt Martha had made it quite clear to Mary that something was wrong with Ralph. Mary knew she had to make her mom believe her.

Mary had not been sleeping when this happened, so her mother couldn't say it was a dream. She went to her mom and told her what had happened. Mrs. Sinclair could see how upset Mary was, so she decided it wouldn't do any harm to ride over and check on Ralph.

She and Mary bundled up against the cold and saddled the horses for the ride over. It was a good thing for Ralph that they did. As they approached, they saw someone on the ground in front of the barn. As they got closer, they saw it was Ralph. His leg was broken, and he couldn't get up by himself. Together, they managed to get him inside and get help.

Ralph had started to the barn to milk the cows, but he slipped and fell on ice. He would have frozen if nobody had come along to help him. After that, Mary's mother believed her little chime child had special powers.

The rest of the winter and the entire springtime passed

without further paranormal incidents. One summer night brought a dramatic change, however. Mary had another experience.

The Sinclair family had gone to bed early that night. A summer storm raged outside, and Mary hadn't been able to sleep because of the thunder. She listened for her big brother Andy to come home and put his horse away, but he didn't come. She thought that he might stay at his girlfriend's house to wait out the storm, but she'd really feel better if she knew he was safe. She always slept better when she knew that all the family was home safe and sound, especially on a stormy night like this one. She lay quietly and worried. The storm showed no signs of letting up. She tossed and turned as the storm continued, pounding the house with wind and rain. The beat of the rain finally made her drowsy, but she was still awake when it happened.

As before, she realized she was not alone in the room. Something was staring at her. She looked at the foot of her bed, and there stood Aunt Martha's ghost. She projected her thoughts very clearly to Mary this time.

"Your brother is hurt," the ghost told her. "He's by the old oak tree down the road near the creek. He needs help now or he will die."

Having completed her message, the ghost faded away in front of Mary's eyes.

Mary never doubted for a second the truth of what Aunt Martha's ghost had said. She jumped out of bed, ran to her parents' room, and woke them.

"Andy needs help right now!" she told them. "He's hurt down by the creek near the oak tree."

Her dad was still groggy from sleep and not too happy about having his sleep interrupted.

"What are you talking about?" he snapped.

She repeated what she had just said.

"You had a nightmare because of this storm," he said. "Now go back to bed."

"No!" Mary insisted. "Aunt Martha came to me and told me!"

"You're not starting that psychic nonsense again, are you?" he asked, sitting up and glaring at her now. "Andy wouldn't come out in a storm like this."

"The storm hit fast," said Mary's mother, sitting up now, too. "Maybe he thought he could beat it and got caught out in it. I think you should go see if something is wrong."

"I'm sure nothing is wrong," Mr. Sinclair insisted. "Andy will be home as soon as the storm is over. Now let's get some sleep!"

"Mary's been right before," Mrs. Sinclair pointed out. "What if something is wrong and you ignore it?"

"I tell you, he's all right!" Mr. Sinclair bellowed, thinking how miserable he would be if he went out in that storm. "He'll be home any time now."

As if to confirm what he said, the sound of hoofbeats approached the house. Mary ran to the window and looked out as the lightning lit up the sky and the yard. She could see clearly, but it was not the sight she wanted to see. Andy's horse ran by the house and headed for the barn, but there was no rider.

"It's Andy's horse, but Andy's not on him!" cried Mary.

This was information that Mr. Sinclair couldn't ignore. He knew something had happened to Andy, and he couldn't waste any time now. He had to go look for him. Mary ran back to the kitchen to look out the back window. Mr. Sinclair got out of bed and dressed quickly for the storm. He hurried to the barn and turned Andy's horse into his stall. He saddled his own horse and rode into the stormy night.

Mary and her mom waited in the kitchen as the storm finally blew itself out. Finally, dawn broke and Mrs. Sinclair made breakfast. They ate in silence as they waited still. At last, a familiar sound came to their ears. A horse was coming! Mary and her mom ran to the door and opened it as Mr. Sinclair came riding up alone. He pulled up the horse, but stayed mounted.

"Did you find him?" asked Mary.

"Is he all right?" Mrs. Sinclair wanted to know before her husband had a chance to speak. He put up his hand to silence them.

"Yes, I found him," he said. " He'll be fine. He's resting over at the doc's house right now. He rode into a limb in the storm. It knocked him off his horse, and he hit his head on a rock when he fell. He was knocked out and bleeding when I found him. The creek had flooded from all the rain, and the water had almost reached him when I got there."

"He could have died!" said Mary.

"Thank God you found him," said Mrs. Sinclair.

"Yeah," said Mr. Sinclair, "the doc said he might not have made it if I hadn't come along when I did."

"Put your horse up while I fix you some breakfast," said Mrs. Sinclair. "You must be starved."

Mr. Sinclair took care of his horse and returned to the house just as his wife put biscuits, eggs, bacon, and hot coffee on the table. While he ate, he told his wife and daughter more details.

"You were right about his thinking he could beat the storm," he told them. "I never would have thought that he'd be out in a storm like that, but he said it came up faster than he thought it would. Mary, he would have died if it hadn't been for you. I would never have gone to look for him. His girlfriend's folks would not have gone to look either because they would have thought he beat the storm and got home safely."

"I had some help from Aunt Martha's ghost and Andy's horse," said Mary, smiling.

"I'll believe you from now on," her father told her.

Mr. Sinclair told that story many times at the old country store where people gathered to shop and visit. Some believed him and some didn't. He really didn't care. He didn't understand it himself. He just knew his little chime child had a special gift.

The Helpful Business Ghost

The owners of the restaurant in this story told this tale to us. They were very sincere, and we didn't doubt them for a second.

Carla and Christy had been friends for several years when they got the idea to open a restaurant together. They didn't have a lot of business experience, but they were both good cooks and good with people. They found a small building in downtown Louisville and went into business, serving lunch only. Everything went well, but it wasn't long until the two owners began to feel that they had a silent, invisible business partner.

The previous owner, a man who had worked well past retirement before he died, had operated a bar at this location. Sometimes the ladies heard a tinkling of glasses in the area where that bar had been, and they felt as though someone was with them as they closed for the day. Sometimes knives that belonged in one area would show up mysteriously in another part of the kitchen. At other times, food would appear in the refrigerator when they were certain they had not put it there themselves. They sometimes joked about whether or not the previous owner approved of two women owning a business where his used to be.

After a few weeks, business began to fall off. Carla and Christy began to worry that perhaps they had made a mistake. They had invested their savings in the restaurant and had nothing to fall back on if this venture failed. They considered cutting their losses and moving on. They could sell the restaurant and find jobs as cooks for other people.

One day after all the customers had gone, Carla and Christy sat down to discuss their future plans seriously and make a decision about what they should do next.

"We're just breaking even," Christy said. "Do you think we should try to stick it out?"

"I'd like to stay," said Carla. "I like working for myself. On the other hand, if we are going to go, it would be better to do it before we get into debt."

"Right," said Christy. "So what do we do? Do we go or do we stay?"

Just then, each woman felt a strong hand on her shoulder. Both heard a male voice whisper distinctly, "Stay!"

Somewhat taken aback by this unexpected advice, the ladies thought it might be a positive sign that things would get better soon. They decided right then and there that they would keep the restaurant open. They considered ways to make business better. They hired a singer and guitarist to play live music, and they implemented some smart advertising plans. The changes worked, and soon business was booming.

The ladies did some research on the previous owner and discovered that he, too, had once experienced doubts about staying in this location. He had decided to stay and had made a success of it.

The ladies still see signs that the late owner is there with them. They feel him standing behind them as they clean the floor, or they find silverware moved around in the kitchen. When this happens, they just smile and say a silent thanks for a business manager that they don't have to pay!

The Banshee

This story happened to neighbors and was retold often on stormy nights when the wind would shriek like a banshee.

The banshee is a ghost that often attaches itself to an Irish family, sometimes following that family to a new country when it moves from Ireland. The banshee appears outside the family's home and wails to let the people know of a coming death. There is much complicated folklore about the banshee and the roles it plays with families, but in the south-central part of Kentucky people connect it to a death warning only.

To encounter a banshee was certainly not an everyday occurrence, but a banshee probably came into the lives of two neighbors who lived along Damron's Creek.

It was a late spring day, and Logan Carter and his son, Clyde, were on their way home after hauling gravel all day. It was almost dark, and the woods along the road were already filling up with shadows. The old truck engine sputtered along, sounding almost as tired as Logan and Clyde felt. Clyde was thinking about the hot supper his mom, Lindy, would have ready. He could almost taste the beans, green onions, hot cornbread, and cold buttermilk. They drove past Dennis Sullivan's house and soon pulled into their own driveway. The younger Carter children were playing in the front yard.

Lindy was outside with her neighbor Maggie Sullivan, the youngest girl in the Sullivan household. They were talking and picking herbs from Lindy's garden just beyond the driveway.

"Just brew these herbs into a tea for your mother," Lindy instructed the girl. "It should help her rest and feel better."

"I hope the tea works," said Maggie. "Momma's awful

sick at her stomach. She can't keep anything down, and she hardly sleeps at all."

"Tell her I'll bring her some chicken soup tomorrow," said Lindy. "That usually stays down when nothing else will. It seems to give a person strength."

Maggie opened her mouth to reply, but she was interrupted by something from the woods that none of them had ever heard before. A sound cut through the warm spring air that chilled their bones. It was the combination of a wail and a scream—a keen, piercing shriek. It left all of them in stunned silence for a moment when it stopped. Then Clyde spoke up.

"What on earth was that?" he asked.

"Maybe a wildcat," said his dad.

"It didn't sound like any wildcat I ever heard," Clyde disagreed.

Maggie turned deathly pale, a look of realization spreading across her face.

"Oh, my Lord!" she said. "It was a banshee! It's come for Momma! I've got to get home. Momma's going to die!"

She started toward the woods, clutching her herbs tightly. Lindy stopped her.

"Wait, child," she called. "You can't go into those woods by yourself! We don't kenow for sure what that was. It could have been an animal that would hurt you. Let Logan drive you home."

Lindy accepted the ride. Tears were streaming down her cheeks when she climbed into the truck beside Logan Carter.

"That wasn't a wildcat," she said to Logan. "The banshee has come for Momma. I need to get home as fast as I can."

The wailing sound rose from the woods again as they drove off. It seemed to come from near the Sullivan place.

The Carter family stood in the yard, watching the truck go down the road.

"What was she talking about?" Clyde asked his mother. "What's a banshee?"

Lindy didn't know much to tell him about it. She knew that the Irish believed it was a sign of death to hear one wail. She knew that the Sullivans were Irish, so maybe the banshee had followed the family to this country. Mrs. Sullivan had talked about it briefly once in a casual conversation.

"I didn't know how much of her story to believe," Lindy told Clyde, "but she certainly believed it."

The trip was short, so Logan was back home in a few minutes. They heard the sound once more as he got out of the truck, and then they all went inside for supper.

"Mrs. Sullivan is in bad shape," Logan told the family as they sat around the supper table. "She sent her thanks for the herbs, though. Maggie was brewing some tea for her when I left. I only stayed a minute to pay my respects since she was so weak, but she said to tell you that she is looking forward to your good chicken soup tomorrow."

Lindy nodded. Chicken soup was a remedy for just about everything.

The shock the family had felt by the shrieking in the woods subdued the conversation as the Carters ate their supper. Their talk was mostly limited to requests for food to be passed. When they finished, Lindy washed the dishes while the others went into the living room and sat quietly. It was Friday night, and things were usually livelier at the Carters' home. Tonight, though, it was as if they didn't want to do anything to call attention to themselves. Something unknown and sinister was out there in the woods, and they wanted no part of it.

They all went to bed early, each one glancing at Logan to make sure he locked the door. They slept fitfully, waking up when they heard the terrible wailing in the distance. They were relieved to notice that the sound was not close to their house.

The next morning after breakfast, Lindy prepared the chicken soup and got ready to take it to Mrs. Sullivan.

"I'll drive you over," said Logan. "I don't want you meeting up with that old wildcat."

"Dad," said Clyde, "you know that wasn't a wildcat!"

"Well," said Logan, "whatever it was, your mother doesn't need to meet up with it while she's carrying that chicken soup."

He and Lindy got in the truck and drove off. The younger children moved closer to Clyde and kept a watchful eye on the woods. No one, including Clyde, wanted to venture too far from the safety of the yard. Finally, they all sat on the porch to wait for their parents to return.

After a while, Logan and Lindy returned with sad news. Mrs. Sullivan had died just before daybreak. It was right after her death that the wailing had stopped.

In the days that followed, the Carters debated whether a wildcat had been in the woods, or whether a banshee had come to take Mrs. Sullivan away to the other side. There was a certain amount of evidence to support both sides, but there was not 100 percent proof for either one.

The Carters never heard the wailing again, so they tried to put the whole thing out of their minds. Sometimes it would come to mind, though, when they were walking through the woods at night, going to the country store, or heading off to visit friends. They all admitted that such thoughts always made them walk a little faster.

The Rock Quarry

The rock quarry was just a few miles down the main road from where we lived. We heard this story as a true happening, but sometimes kids wondered if the old folks made it up to scare them away.

In central Kentucky, an old rock quarry stood abandoned with a few feet of water covering the bottom. Once productive, it was now an empty, eerie-looking place. There were several "No Trespassing" signs around the boundaries, but the site had few visitors now.

Three neighborhood boys, Derek, Aaron, and Donnie, thought the old rock quarry was mysterious and irresistible. They had been told time and again by their parents to stay away from the place because it could be dangerous, but the warnings fell on deaf ears.

"Why do you want to play there?" their parents wanted

to know. "There's no fish in the water, so you can't go fishing. And the water is muddy and the bottom has sharp rocks, so you can't go swimming. What's the attraction?"

The truth was that the boys were not interested in fishing or swimming. They were often picked on by the other boys because they liked to read or sit around doing nothing instead of playing sports, and they wanted someplace to get away from the bullies. They liked to sit on the bank at the quarry and throw rocks into the water. They liked to read stories of monsters, so it was easy to imagine that some killer monster lurked in the scum and mud at the bottom of the quarry. They made up stories about the monster to see who could outdo the other in telling about the monster's escapades. They had formed a secret club, called the Monster Hunters, and they thought that the quarry was the perfect place to meet. It was only five miles down the road from where they lived, and they could easily reach it on their bicycles without being detected.

One day after a particularly hard PE class where they had been ridiculed by the usual bullies, the three boys could hardly wait to get off by themselves at the quarry. It was peaceful there, and they could forget about the sweaty, smelly gym. Here they didn't have to compete against anybody. Here it was just the three of them against the quarry monster, and they were always the winners.

The boys parked their bikes behind some bushes so they could not be seen by the road, and made their way to their favorite spot on the bank. They sat looking at the smooth surface of the water and talked about what the quarry must have been like when men and machines moved the rocks. Donnie stood up and walked right up to the water.

"Mom said that a girl was supposed to have drowned here while the quarry was in operation," he said to the other boys.

"Yeah, I heard that, too," said Derek. "Her boyfriend got mad at her and pushed her in the water."

Aaron was listening intently to his two friends, so none of them heard the noise in the bushes behind them. None of them noticed that two boys from PE had followed them when class was over and had been listening to their conversation. Now the two intruders dashed up behind the boys before they knew what was happening. They shoved Donnie into the murky water and threw a couple of rocks at Aaron and Derek before jumping on their bicycles and taking off.

"Help! I can't swim!" cried Donnie, sinking under the surface.

His two friends wanted to help, but they didn't know how to swim very well, either. They stood there watching as their friend surfaced once and went down again. Then Derek sprang into action. He grabbed a limb that was on the ground near the bank. Aaron grabbed on, too, and together they carried it to the water's edge.

As Donnie came up again, he managed to grab hold of the limb they extended to him. Derek and Aaron doubted that they had the strength to pull Donnie from the water, but they knew it was his only chance.

Much to their amazement, the task proved to be fairly easy. It was almost as if someone were swimming and pushing Donnie along. One last tug and Donnie was on the bank, drenched in muddy water, but safe and sound.

They all sat on the bank quietly for a moment to catch their breath.

"Wow," said Derek, "I wasn't sure we were going to make it at first."

"Me either," said Aaron.

"It was the strangest thing," said Donnie. "I thought I was going to die for sure. Then I saw a white face in the water. Next, I felt hands holding me up and pushing me toward the bank while you guys were pulling me in. As I landed on the bank, whatever was pushing stopped and disappeared."

"It must have been that girl who drowned," said Aaron. "You know, the one they never found!"

It was getting late, so the boys left the quarry and hurried home. Of course, the muddy clothes betrayed their secret meeting place to their parents. Again, they forbade the boys to go there, but the boys didn't obey for long. This time, they had a special purpose for going.

They picked a beautiful bouquet of flowers and placed them on the bank. They threw a few flowers into the water, in case the girl really was in her watery grave there.

Donnie whispered, "Thank you!"

As they turned to go, they heard a splash in the water in the center of the quarry. They looked just in time to see a white figure go under the water. Then all was still.

The Wet Doll

When we were young children, we did not have an abundance of toys like kids do today. That made whatever toys we had extra special to us. A neighbor lady, Miss Foley, told this story, but other people had their own versions, too.

Old stories that were passed from one generation to another often included surprising tales of toys with special powers.

The Gill family—Ben, Bonnie, and young Charlotte and Calvin—moved into a log house on the banks of the Cumberland River. They had inherited the place from Bonnie's aunt, who had raised her family in the old house. The inheritance couldn't have come at a better time for the Gills, because their house had been burned when lightning struck it and they had been left with no place to live. They had lost everything in the fire—furniture, the children's toys, everything—and they had no money with which to replace their belongings.

It was another stroke of good luck for the Gills that Bonnie's aunt had left some furniture in the house. Neighbors and other relatives gave them clothes, kitchen items, and bedding to help them set up housekeeping in the new place. Little Calvin made himself a fishing pole, but Charlotte had nothing special to play with. Bonnie and Ben told the children not to play near the river without them, so playtime by the water was limited.

Several days after they moved in, it rained so hard that the children's play area was even more restricted. They couldn't play outside, so they were bored and moped around the house until Calvin got an idea.

"Momma, may we play in the attic?" he asked.

Bonnie thought that was a wonderful idea, so she told them to go ahead.

Calvin and Charlotte hurriedly climbed the stairs and opened the attic door. They were greeted by a stuffy smell, but they ignored it and turned on the light by the door. As the light flooded the attic room, they were surprised to see several boxes lined up against the back wall. The excited children rushed to the boxes as though they were treasure chests. In the first box they found old clothes, blankets, and quilts. The next box contained old clothes and photo albums. The box after that held old dishes. Then they opened a box filled with old toys! Calvin took out two balls and some toy soldiers. Charlotte removed a toy tea set and a rag doll. When they had finished looking in all the boxes, they realized that the rainy day had passed without their hardly noticing.

When Bonnie called them for supper, the children decided to bring some of the toys downstairs to play with after the meal was over. Calvin chose the soldiers, and Charlotte picked up the doll.

Calvin was already heading for the stairs when Charlotte began screaming. He turned to see his sister throw the doll to the floor and begin to cry.

"What's wrong?" he asked. "What's the matter with you?"

"The doll!" she sobbed. "It opened its eyes and stared at me. Then it reached out one arm!"

"It couldn't do that," Calvin told her. "It's a rag doll. Its eyes don't open, and its arms don't bend. It was just the shadows playing tricks on you."

Their mother had heard her daughter's scream and had made it to the top of the stairs by then. Charlotte ran to her, still crying.

"What on earth is going on up here?" Bonnie asked the children.

Charlotte repeated her story while Calvin stood there shaking his head. He picked up the doll and handed it to his mother.

"See?" he said. "There's nothing wrong with it. It's just an old rag doll. Charlotte's crazy."

"Hush that," Bonnie told Calvin. "Now both of you come on down to supper. Calvin, bring the doll with your soldiers so we can take a look at it later."

Calvin followed his mother and sister downstairs. He held the doll and soldiers out for his dad to see. Ben glanced at them and told Calvin to put them in the living room until after supper. When Calvin returned and took his place at the table, the family ate, mostly in silence.

After the dishes were done, Bonnie joined the rest of the family in the living room. They were all looking at the toys. Ben was pointing out to Charlotte that the rag doll was normal.

"I wonder who had this doll before I found it," said Charlotte.

"It must have belonged to your cousin Emma," said

Bonnie. "She drowned near here in the river when she was just a little girl. She was a sweet child. I am sure she wouldn't mind your playing with her doll."

The family experienced no other strange occurrence surrounding the doll, so Charlotte gradually set her fears aside. She named the doll Emma, after her dead cousin. She always kept the doll with her.

One day, Ben took Calvin with him to help a neighbor do some work on the next farm. About midafternoon, Bonnie heard a rumble of thunder and remembered that she had heard on the radio that they might have severe storms that night. If they did, the power might go out and they might need to light the lamps. She would need oil for the lamps, so she called Charlotte and sent her off to the store to get some.

"Stay on the path by the river, but don't go near the bank," Bonnie told her. "Hurry and don't stop to play."

"Okay," promised Charlotte, as she hurried down the path.

Bonnie saw that the sky was darkening, so she rushed to get supper cooked. She kept an eye on the cloud and an eye on the path, hoping that Charlotte would get home before the storm hit. The clouds began to move faster, and Bonnie began to worry because Charlotte was not home yet. Then she heard the front door open.

"Charlotte, is that you?" she called.

"It's us," called Ben. "We quit work early because of the storm."

"Did you see Charlotte coming up the path?" she asked.

Calvin and Ben both shook their heads.

"Where'd she go?" asked Ben.

"I sent her to the store for some oil, but she hasn't come back yet. She's had plenty of time. I'm getting worried."

"The cloud's so close, they probably kept her at the store," Ben said. "I'll go over and get her when the storm's over."

Just then, the rain arrived, and the three sat in the kitchen, thinking that Ben must be right about the storekeeper not letting Charlotte go out in the storm. Any adult would certainly keep a child inside. Still, they waited and silently worried. The wind thrashed the trees around and the lightning danced at the windows.

The lightning lit up a chair by the window, and Calvin noticed Charlotte had left her doll there. He walked over and picked it up.

"Look at this!" he exclaimed. "The doll's soaking wet!"

"Is the window open?" asked Ben.

"No," said Calvin. "And everything else is dry."

Calvin held the doll out away from him, and they could all see water dripping from her. They couldn't imagine why the doll would be wet.

"It's a message," said Calvin. "It's trying to tell us that Charlotte is caught out in the storm!"

It seemed like a far-fetched idea to Ben Gill, but he had a nagging feeling that something was wrong. He couldn't take any chances. He grabbed his raincoat and ran down the path. He had gone only a short way when he saw the oil can by the pathway.

"Charlotte," he called. "It's Daddy! Where are you?"

"Here," she called. "Help me!"

He ran to the riverbank and saw Charlotte clinging to a limb that had broken from a tree. She reached out one hand and he took it.

"Give me your other hand," he said.

She reached the other hand, and he pulled her from the water.

"You're okay now," he told her. "I've got you."

"Oh, Daddy!" she cried. "I was afraid you wouldn't come. The storm caught me before I could get home."

"What happened?" Ben asked her.

"The wind blew me down, so I grabbed onto that tree and pulled myself up. I was holding on, but the limb broke and I fell into the river. I kept holding on, but sometimes my hands would slip off and I'd have to grab on again. It was the strangest thing, though. Something held me up in the water each time until I got my grip again."

"Well, you're safe now," he said. "We're going home."

He took Charlotte's hand and led her to the path. With his other hand, he picked up the oil can, and they hurried home as fast as the storm would allow.

Bonnie quickly helped her daughter change into dry clothes, and she made some hot chocolate for all of them. The storm continued outside, but they were all safe now, thanks to Emma. They told Charlotte how the wet doll had made them realize she needed help.

"Did you fall into the river right there at the bend?" asked Bonnie.

"Yes," said Charlotte.

"And you felt like something was holding you up?" Bonnie continued.

"Yes," Charlotte said again.

"That's odd," said Bonnie. "That's just where your little cousin Emma drowned years ago! Maybe that Emma gave you something besides giving you her doll. Maybe she held you up."

"Was my doll really dripping wet?" asked Charlotte.

They all nodded, but Charlotte went to her doll to see for herself. She picked up the doll and then looked at the family with a puzzled look on her face.

"Are you sure she was wet?" she asked. "She's bone dry now!"

As far as the Gill family was concerned, a miracle had happened that day, and they never looked for any other answer.

The Red Thing

This story was always hard to believe, but great-great-uncle Lightel Simpson told it as the truth.

Lightel Simpson had completed a successful day of deer hunting in the Kentucky backwoods and was a little tired from the day's activities. He had gutted the big buck he had shot and had hung it on the branch of a large tree in the back of his cabin. He figured he would cut it up after he rested a bit and ate a bite of supper.

He put his prize hunting dogs in the pen out back and fed them their supper first. Then he heated up some stew and cornbread and ate by himself.

The dusk deepened and the moon came up. Lightel decided to relax a bit and let his food digest before he cut up the buck, so he took his guitar and moved out onto the front porch. He started strumming softly, but he suddenly was overcome by a most uneasy feeling. He stopped playing his guitar and sat quietly, listening. Then he realized what the problem was. The woods around his cabin were totally silent. The crickets, frogs, and all the forest creatures were not moving or making a sound. That was a sure sign of danger close by.

Suddenly, the silence was broken by Lightel's hunting dogs whimpering and running out from behind the house with their tails tucked! They dashed under the floor of the cabin and stopped whimpering, falling as silent as everything in the woods. Lightel was amazed. He had never known his dogs to dig out of their pen before. He laid his guitar on the porch beside his chair and stood up, still listening for any sound.

Then he heard what he wished he hadn't heard. His skin crawled as the air was pierced by a screech like nothing Lightel had ever heard from human or animal. It came from behind the cabin in the vicinity of the buck. Then the noise started to move toward the end of the cabin. He was too frightened to move.

In the moonlight, Lightel saw something stop at the end

of the porch. It looked red and smelled bad, and it walked upright. Its eyes glowed red, too, as they focused on him and started slowly around the porch. It threw back its head and let out another blood-curdling screech.

Lightel thought he could not move, but the last screech pumped adrenalin to his legs, and he lunged for his cabin door. He got inside, closed the door, and bolted it just as the red thing came up on the porch. Lightel's escape had been a narrow one, and even then he was not sure he was out of danger. The cabin walls and doors were thick. Lightel prayed they would hold the thing outside. He crouched beside the door and listened to the thing scrape its claws across the wood, but fortunately the door held. The creature scraped and scraped, and then paced back and forth across the porch. It walked upright most of the time, but sometimes Lightel could hear it walking on all fours.

The night crept by and the red thing stayed on the porch. The dogs stayed under the house and never uttered a single bark. Lightel got his loaded gun and held it across his lap, but he had the feeling it wouldn't offer much protection if the creature got inside.

Finally, mercifully, the sun came up. It was not a welcome sight for the red thing. It let out another screech that rattled the small windows of the cabin. Then it moved off the porch and vanished into the woods.

Lightel waited to go outside until he heard his dogs come out from under the cabin. He figured they would know if the red thing had gone or not. He found his guitar untouched on the porch, but the buck he had hung in the tree was completely devoured. He was grateful that there was no sign of the red thing.

Lightel told friends and family about his frightening ordeal, but nobody believed him. Some suggested that he must have sampled some moonshine after he ate his stew and cornbread. He had not had anything to drink, though. He knew what he had seen.

Only one other old-timer said he had heard stories of red things that lived deep in the woods and hardly ever came out. He said it only happened if their food supply got really low. Nobody believed him either, except Lightel.

For the rest of his life, Lightel made sure his chores were done and that he was safely inside before dark. People could laugh at him if they wanted to. He was not going to take any chances. He was thankful that he never heard that awful screech or saw the red thing again.

Howard's Home

Roberta's Uncle Josh always had dogs on the farm. He told this and other dog stories that always fascinated us.

Some of us believe that dogs go to heaven as people do, and that they can return and appear to the living.

Howard was a little black mutt, a dog of mixed breed. He did not come from a royal canine bloodline; he came from the pound as a rescue dog to four-year-old Mattie Granger and her family. From the day they brought him home, Howard made it clear that his heart belonged to Mattie. She was equally clear about her love for Howard. She named him Howard after her best friend who had moved away. Howard was happy to take over that role.

Mattie and Howard liked to play ball in the backyard. When the ball would roll into the woods behind the house, Howard would go fetch it and bring it back. One day Mattie threw it so hard that it rolled into the woods out of sight. Howard dashed into the woods, and Mattie ran after him. Mr. Granger happened to see them and called them both back.

"Don't go into the woods, Mattie," he said. "It would be easy to get lost in there. Mr. Phillips owns them, and he hasn't cleared out any trees in years. Any kind of dangerous animal could be in there. Plus, I know Mr. Phillips has a big dog. I want you to play in your own yard."

"Okay, Daddy," promised Mattie.

Howard made no response. He wouldn't have promised to stay in the yard even if he could. The woods were a wondrous place to the little dog. There was space to run unseen among the brush and trees, and there were things to chase!

One day Mattie came down with a cold and couldn't come out to play ball with Howard. Howard stayed inside and kept her company for a while, but when she went to sleep, Howard scratched on the door for Mrs. Granger to let him out. She thought he would soon be back at the door wanting to come back inside, but that was not what Howard had in mind.

The little dog headed straight for the woods. He was sure he could find something to do there, and he was right. First thing, up jumped a rabbit, and the chase was on! To Howard, it was a wonderful game.

Howard kept in sight of the rabbit until he found himself in unfamiliar territory. Suddenly, the rabbit turned into some bushes and was gone. Howard stopped, a little confused. Just then, a noise in the bushes caught his attention. He thought it was the rabbit, so he sensed no danger. Howard watched as a huge dog twice his size emerged from the bushes and charged at him. Howard was not a fighter, but he tried to defend himself. His efforts were useless, though, because the attacking dog was too big and too mean to handle. He went for Howard's throat and made the kill. Then he went on his way to Mr. Phillips's house, where he lived.

Mrs. Granger was busy and did not notice right away that Howard had not come back yet. Mattie woke up and asked for him, so Mrs. Granger went to the back door and called him. She expected him to come running like he always did, but this time there was no sign of the little black dog.

"Mommy," said Mattie, starting to get out of bed. "I'll go look for him."

"No, Mattie," said her mother. "You have to stay in bed until you feel better. Howard is probably off chasing a rabbit somewhere, but I'll have your dad go look for him if he isn't home by suppertime."

Howard still had not come home by suppertime. Mattie felt well enough to come down to the table for supper, but her mother still would not let her go outside. When the meal was over, Mr. Granger went into the woods to look for Howard.

"Howard!" he called again and again, but there was no response. Darkness was settling over the woods now, so Mr. Granger gave up the search and went back home.

"I'm sure he'll show up in the morning," he told Mattie. "He's probably rambling around in the woods."

Mattie went to the door and called for Howard before she went to bed, but all was silent in the yard and the woods beyond. She hoped her dad was right about Howard's coming home in the morning. She went to bed and finally fell sleep.

During the night, a thunderstorm passed over the Granger house. The wind howled and the rain beat down on the yard and woods. The thunder and wind woke Mattie, and immediately she thought of little Howard out in the storm. She pulled back the cover and got out of bed. She stuck her feet into her little house shoes and went down to the kitchen. She opened the back door and called and called for Howard, but he didn't come.

"I've got to go find him," she told herself. "He's afraid of storms."

And out the door she went, straight into the woods. She walked farther and farther among the trees, and there she saw Howard's body on the ground. She sat down beside him and began to cry. She began to feel a chill and started to cough, but she had no idea of how to get home. She began to get very sleepy.

Back at the Granger house, the storm woke Mrs. Granger. She went to Mattie's room to check on her and discovered she was not in bed. She looked in the bathroom, but Mattie was not there, either.

"Wake up!" she called to her husband, running back into their room. "Mattie's not in bed!"

They both hurried down to the kitchen and saw the back door slightly open.

"Oh, my Lord!" cried Mrs. Granger. "She's gone out in the storm to find that dog! She'll catch her death of cold. We've got to find her."

She was interrupted by a bark coming from the edge of the woods. She and her husband both looked out the door.

"Look at that," said Mr. Granger. "Howard's home!"

He opened the door wider and called to him.

"Come here, boy! Come on in!"

Howard made no move toward the house. He would bark, go into the woods, come out and bark again.

"I think he wants you to go with him," said Mrs. Granger. "Maybe he knows where Mattie is!"

"I'm going to follow him," said Mr. Granger, pulling on his raincoat. "I'll be back as soon as I can."

Mrs. Granger watched Howard and her husband disappear into the woods. She stood at the kitchen door and waited as the minutes ticked by. The thunder and wind had passed on, but the rain had stayed on to continue its steady beat. She could see most of the yard from the porch light, but nothing moved out there.

She left the door and put on some water to boil for tea.

When her husband found Mattie, she would need something to warm her up. She made strong coffee for herself and her husband. With that accomplished, she went back to the door. It seemed forever before she saw her husband emerge from the woods, carrying their daughter in his arms. Howard was not with them. She thought that was odd, but she now focused her attention on her child. She took off Mattie's wet clothes, put a clean, warm gown on her, and wrapped her in a blanket. Her head was hot with fever, so Mrs. Granger gave her some tea and put her to bed.

Mr. Granger changed into some warm, dry clothes and sat down with his wife to drink a cup of the steaming coffee.

"Where's Howard?" she asked.

"He's dead," Mr. Granger answered softly.

"Dead?" gasped Mrs. Granger. "What happened?"

"It didn't just happen," Mr. Granger explained. "He's been dead awhile. It looked like he got in a fight with a big dog, probably the Phillips's dog. He was back in the woods off the path, and I found Mattie beside his body."

"But he was clearly leading you!" exclaimed Mrs. Granger.

"I know," said Mr. Granger. "He seemed as alive as you and me! I thought he was alive until I caught sight of Mattie beside his body there on the ground. The Howard I'd been following vanished then. I wouldn't have found Mattie so soon without his help."

Later that day, while Mattie was recovering from her ordeal, Mr. Granger went back into the woods with Howard's favorite blanket. He wrapped the body of the little dog in the blanket and carried it back to the backyard. He dug a grave and buried the family's best friend. This time Howard was home for good.

Ghost by the Tree

Roberta's Uncle Lawrence liked this story and often told it when we gathered for storytelling.

When Tim Dutton was a teenager in the 1900s, he moved with his family to a western Kentucky farm that they had bought at auction. He wasn't too pleased about the move because it meant living farther away from his friends and the small town where they had been living. There had been all sorts of things to do in town, but in the country it seemed he always had to be doing some kind of chore or dealing with a problem of some kind.

From the first day the family had moved to the farm, there had been a problem with the cows.

They didn't want to come from the pasture to the barn for milking at the end of the day. For the first two days, Tim's dad rounded them up and brought them to the barn, but then he decided it would be a perfect chore for Tim. Tim totally disagreed.

"I don't know why they can't come up by themselves," he grumbled. "We should just leave them out there until they do!"

"I can't work by their schedule," said Mr. Dutton. "It's

strange, though. That big oak tree is the only shade, but they don't gather under it. They don't even like to walk by it."

"Maybe they're spooked by the tree," Tim's younger sister, Ester, suggested.

"That's silly," said Tim. "Why would they be spooked by an oak tree?"

"Haven't you heard?" she asked. "A man hanged himself in that tree. He lost his farm and then he lost his mind. So he hanged himself."

"You're making that up," accused Tim.

"I am not," she insisted. "People have seen his ghost standing by the tree late in the afternoon 'cause that's the time he did it."

"Where did you hear that?" asked the father.

"At school," she said. "Several people told me when they found out we had moved here."

"I think maybe they were playing a little joke on you," said her father.

"They weren't kidding," she said. "They were serious."

Tim and his father shook their heads and disregarded her explanation for the lingering cows. Ester shrugged her shoulders and went on about her playing. If they didn't want to hear the truth, it was all right with her. They could find out for themselves.

Tim thought the cows lingered because they liked grazing in the fresh air. Even cows would not like to be shut up in a barn when they could be free outside.

On one particular day, however, Tim's father did not

take into consideration what the cows might want. It looked like rain was moving in, and he wanted the chores done now. It was time to feed and milk the cows, so he told Tim to hurry up and bring them to the barn.

Tim strolled through the pasture, passed by the oak tree, and started down the hill where the cows were grazing. He hated to admit it to himself, but, as he had passed the tree, he had gotten the eeriest feeling that he wasn't alone. Low thunder caused him to look up, and he glimpsed someone standing beside the tree. He blinked and looked again. Whoever it was had gone.

"I get it," he said to himself. "My sister sneaked down to the tree to scare me."

He stared at the tree to see if he could catch her hiding, but as he looked he heard her call him from the yard.

"Did you see something by the tree?" she called.

"Of course not!" he lied.

He couldn't let her know she'd been right. She'd be so smug about it that he'd never live it down.

She laughed and went back to her playing.

Tim decided that he must have seen a shadow. Whatever it was, it made him uneasy. For once, he herded the cows to the barn quickly, feeling very relieved to be safely back from the field.

Everybody gathered inside for supper, and a soft rain set in, giving a cozy feeling to the family inside. Tim managed to put the disturbing experience at the tree out of his mind until the next afternoon when it was time to go get the cows again.

As he approached the tree, he warned himself not to imagine things. Then, suddenly, the man was beside the tree again. Tim had no idea where he had come from. One second the tree was normal. The next second, the man was there.

"Hey, Mister!" Tim called to the man.

The man didn't answer. Instead, he vanished as mysteriously as he had come.

"My sister's tale is causing me to see things," he said to himself. "It's the power of suggestion."

He hurried the cows to the barn as fast as he could, but he saw nothing else that day.

During school the next day, Tim told his two cousins, Hollis and Elvin, about what he had seen. He was surprised when they told him they had heard the same tale his sister had told. They told him they didn't believe it, though.

"Dead people don't come back," said Hollis.

"You were imagining things," said Elvin.

It annoyed Tim that they didn't take him seriously.

"I'll prove that something's there," he told them. "Come over after school and go with me to get the cows. I'll bet you two dollars that something is by the tree."

"You're on!" said Elvin.

"Right," said Hollis.

They all shook hands to seal the bet.

His cousins hadn't yet arrived by the time his father told Tim to go get the cows, so he had to cross the pasture alone. He looked at the tree as he passed by, but no man appeared. He saw his two cousins in the distance coming down the road. He knew they'd be there soon. Now money was riding on this bet, and Tim did not intend to lose. His cousins were going to see a ghost by the tree, even if he had to pretend to be the ghost himself.

He ducked behind the tree and stepped out as the cousins got close. They stopped in their tracks, and Tim could see their faces turn white. It was obvious that they were really frightened.

"He was right," gasped Hollis. "It's a ghost!"

"Yeah," said Elvin, "but he said there was only one ghost. Why are there two? Let's get out of here!"

They turned and ran back the way they had come without looking back.

Tim was puzzled. He couldn't figure what they were talking about when they said two ghosts.

Tim looked at the other side of the tree, and there stood the ghostly figure he had seen before.

Tim raced down the hill and rounded up the cows faster than he had ever done before. Hollis and Elvin were waiting at the house for him when he got there. They were all so frightened that they agreed to call off the bet.

Mr. Dutton wasn't quite convinced that they had seen a ghost, but after some consideration he decided to turn the cows into another pasture. Tim thought it was the best decision his father had ever made. The cows seemed to agree. From then on, they came to the barn by themselves when they were called at feeding and milking time.

A Boyfriend's Warning

The Gentrys were Roberta's relatives on her mother's side. One of the Gentry girls told this story at one of our neighborhood storytelling get-togethers.

Ruby and Doug had been in love since grade school. It started as puppy love, but it grew into a strong relationship, with each completely devoted to the other. Doug gave Ruby an engagement ring when they graduated from high school, but they didn't set a wedding date because Doug had received his draft notice and had to go fight in World War II.

Ruby thought they should be married before Doug left for training, but Doug wanted to wait until he returned.

"I don't want us to marry and then have to separate when I have to go off right away. When we get married, I want us to be together forever. I want to be there to take care of you always."

"You always take good care of me," said Ruby. "I have a feeling we shouldn't wait."

Doug, along with Ruby's parents, convinced her that it would be best to wait and get married when Doug had served his time and got discharged. When they said good-bye, Ruby had a terrible feeling that she would never see Doug again.

After Doug left, Ruby was lonely. She decided to get a job and save some money so that she and Doug would have a little nest egg to start out on when they got married. There weren't many jobs available, but Ruby was lucky to find employment. She was hired as a waitress in the Magnolia Café, and she was good at her job because she liked meeting people.

The weeks turned into months, and she and Doug wrote to each other faithfully. Slowly, Ruby was able to push her fear of never seeing him again into the back of her mind.

Then Doug's letters stopped. The gnawing fear came back in full force. Ruby's parents and friends tried to give her reasons not to worry. They reminded her of top security in certain locations and that mail was censored or not forwarded at all. In her heart, though, she knew they were wrong. Then her fear was confirmed. A telegram informed Ruby that Doug had been killed in action.

The body was too mutilated to be viewed, so he was buried in a closed coffin. Ruby had been right. She never saw Doug again after the day they said good-bye.

Ruby was inconsolable. Why hadn't she believed her feelings? Why hadn't she insisted that they be married? At least that way she would have been his wife for a little while. Maybe they would even have had a child. But now she was completely alone. Her parents couldn't get through to Ruby through her grief. She felt she no longer had a reason to live. She wanted people to leave her alone. She only went out of the house to go to work.

A year passed and Ruby refused to date anyone. She still wore her engagement ring, and as far as she was concerned, her heart would always belong to Doug.

Then one day, David Roberts walked into the Magnolia Café and into Ruby's life. He was an ex-Marine just intending to pass through, but Ruby caught his eye. Right on the spot, he decided to stay for a while. He asked Ruby for a date, and to everybody's surprise, she accepted! Even more surprising, Ruby took off her engagement ring and left it on her dresser. For the next few weeks, David and Ruby were a steady item.

"I've met the perfect man," she told her parents one night. "David is the man I want to marry."

"Honey," her mother said, "nobody is perfect. You hardly know David."

"Maybe you should get to know him better before you think about marrying him," her father told her.

"I know him well enough," said Ruby, "and David doesn't want to wait."

"Well, sleep on it," her mother suggested.

Ruby didn't answer, but went on up to bed. Her parents worried. Something didn't feel quite right.

The next morning, Ruby walked into the kitchen where her parents were getting ready to eat breakfast. She held out the engagement ring that Doug had given her.

"Did you put this on my pillow, Mom?" she asked.

"Heavens, no!" answered her mother, surprised at the question.

"Did you do it, Daddy?" she asked.

"You know I would never come into your room while you were sleeping and do a thing like that!" he said.

"It was on my dresser when I went to bed," she said.

"During the night, I had a dream of Doug. He was holding the ring and shaking his head no! When I woke up, the ring was on my pillow! How could that be?"

Ruby sat down, pale and shaken.

"Maybe it's a sign that you should have second thoughts about marrying David right away," said her mother.

"I agree with your mother," said her father.

"Don't start that again," said Ruby, getting up and hurrying to her room.

She returned the ring to her dresser and got ready for a date with David. When he picked her up later, she left with him without saying anything to her parents.

Ruby returned late that night. Her parents were still up, pretending to watch a late movie on TV. Actually, they were worried sick about her. They saw right away that she had been crying.

"What's wrong?" asked her father. "What happened?"

"David and I had a fight," sobbed Ruby. "He wanted to know how much money I have saved. He wanted us to run off tonight and get married. I just couldn't do that. He said he would give me until tomorrow, and that it will be all over between us if I won't marry him then. He's leaving town and he wants us to go right away. What am I going to do?"

"One thing you're going to do is to let me do some checking on him," declared her father. "There is something wrong about this man. He is rushing you too much!"

"Do go up and get some sleep," said her mother. "We'll see what happens tomorrow."

Nobody in the house slept well that night. Ruby was still upset and uncertain, and her parents were worried that she would do the wrong thing.

The next morning, Ruby came down to breakfast carrying the ring again. Her parents were surprised. Ruby was smiling!

"I couldn't fall asleep for a long time," she told them, "but I finally did, and slept soundly. When I awoke, I saw the ring on my pillow again. I thought maybe you were right, Mom. Maybe Doug was trying to tell me something. He told me he'd always take care of me. I think this was his way of telling me that David is the wrong man for me. If it wasn't for seeing the ring, I might have run away with David. Now I know he is not the right man for me."

When David called that morning, Ruby told him she would not be going away with him. Angrily, he slammed down the phone. She never heard from him again.

Her father checked on David anyway. He learned that David Roberts had been dishonorably discharged from the Marines, and that he was wanted by the police in another state for beating his ex-wife. Maybe Doug saw this from his perspective in the next world and could warn Ruby only by moving the engagement ring he had given her.

The Ghost of the Blackberry Patch

No one teller comes to mind for this story. We usually heard it when a group of women would tell stories while sitting under a shade tree, breaking green beans.

The biggest treat for many people in farm country in Kentucky is blackberries. They are delicious freshly picked or cooked into jam or jelly, or baked into pies and cobblers. They grow abundantly in berry patches, and people pick them both for their own use and for selling to those who are not able to get out and pick themselves. Picking blackberries was a sure way for children to make some money.

Along with the good blackberries, however, could come some bad things.

A tale is told by local people about a crazy man who had escaped from an insane asylum and was believed to live in a cave somewhere deep in the woods. Nobody really believed it, but it was a good story to scare little kids to keep them from wandering into the woods to play. Of course, there were real things to scare them, too. There were thorns that would scratch painfully if the berry pickers were not careful. Chiggers and snakes liked to live in blackberry patches, so pickers had to watch out for them, too. Berry pickers usually wore long sleeves and long pants to protect themselves from bites. Some put kerosene (like they used in their lamps) around their wrists and ankles so the odor would repel chiggers and even snakes. The wise ones wore shoes and did not venture into the blackberry patches with bare feet. Parents who allowed children to pick berries alone always warned them to watch out for snakes and not get bit.

Common snakes in Kentucky were black snakes, cow snakes, rattlesnakes, and copperheads. Snakes like to hide among the berries and wait for birds to swoop down to get berries to eat. Then the snakes would strike. Berry pickers needed a keen eye to spot the snakes and not become a snake-bite victim. Still, people took a chance and picked the berries.

Maggie Gammon awoke one summer morning and asked her mother if she could go berry picking that day. Maggie had seen a dress in the Sears and Roebuck catalog that she wanted to order. She had been saving up for it and almost had enough.

"Honey, I've got to wash today, so I can't go with you. I think you'd better wait. I don't like for you to go alone," her mother told her.

"But, Momma!" Maggie protested. "Mrs. Pennington is expecting company. She always makes pies when she has company. I know she'll buy some berries from me! It will be enough for me to buy that dress. Please, Momma!" she begged.

Mrs. Gammon hesitated. She didn't like to send her daughter out alone, but Maggie was always careful. And she was so eager to get that dress.

"Please, Momma!" Maggie said again. "I promise I'll be careful!"

"Oh, all right," said Mrs. Gammon, giving in to her daughter's pleas. "Don't go into the woods, though. The dogs keep barking at something in there. I looked, but I couldn't see anything. I am going to have your father check it out."

"Do you think they see the crazy man?" joked Maggie.

"Very funny!" laughed Mrs. Gammon. "Just get on your way before I change my mind!"

Maggie gave her mother a big hug.

"Thank you! Thank you! Thank you!" she said. "I won't be gone long."

She grabbed her bucket and ran out the door, never to return home again.

Mrs. Gammon washed the family's clothes as she had planned. Then she carried them outside and hung them on the clothesline to dry.

"I wonder what's keeping that child so long," thought Mrs. Gammon. "I could use some help hanging these clothes."

The sun climbed higher in the sky, and the temperature rose toward the upper nineties. The forecast was for a hot day. Mrs. Gammon finished hanging the clothes by herself, wiped the sweat from her brow, and began to cook the noon meal. Mr. Gammon, who had been working in the fields, came in to eat.

"Where's Maggie?" he asked.

"She went blackberry picking," said Mrs. Gammon. "I'm getting a little worried. She should have been back a long time ago."

"Do you think she might have gone to sell them to someone?" asked Mr. Gammon.

"She's never done that without coming home to tell me," said Mrs. Gammon.

"I'll walk down to the blackberry patch and take a look around," said Mr. Gammon.

"No," said Mrs. Gammon. "You eat your dinner so you can get back to work. I'll go. I know where she usually picks. Lord, I hope she's not snake bit!"

Mrs. Gammon hurried to the patch by the woods where her daughter always loved to go.

"Maggie!" she called. "Where are you? Come on in! It's time to eat."

There was no answer. The woods were silent, too. Mrs. Gammon saw no sign of a snake, but she noticed that the grass was smashed down as if something had been dragged into the woods. Her heart nearly stopped when she saw Maggie's empty bucket on the ground. Right beside it was one of Maggie's shoes.

Mrs. Gammon ran to the house, screaming for her husband. He ran out to see what was wrong. She collapsed into his arms, crying.

"Maggie's gone!" she sobbed. "Something dragged her into the woods! I found her shoe and empty bucket!"

"Now calm down," he told her. "Go inside and call the sheriff. Wait for him here. I'm going to look for her."

Her husband ran toward the blackberry patch by the woods while Mrs. Gammon dialed the sheriff's number. A quick look around the blackberry patch gave Mr. Gammon no information about his daughter. He turned and headed into the woods. He saw the shoe of Maggie's that his wife had seen. He could see where bushes had been broken and pushed down, as if someone had been dragged into the woods. He struggled to fight down his fear, but he knew there had definitely been something in the blackberry patch much more dangerous than a snake.

The sheriff arrived with some men, and they proceeded

to search the whole area. Maggie's other shoe was found on the ground at the edge of a cliff above a creek. There were no other clues about Maggie's whereabouts. The men searched the woods and down along the creek, but there was no trace of the missing girl. They continued the search for days, but they had little hope of finding her now. Some of the searchers swore that they heard something following along beside them while they were searching, but the invisible thing never materialized. Finally the search was called off.

Mrs. Gammon refused to believe that her daughter was gone forever. She kept busy during the day. In the daylight hours, she could pretend that Maggie was off visiting her friends, but it was different when darkness settled over the woods and the blackberry patch. She felt so guilty about letting Maggie go out alone that morning! She would leave the house at night and go to the blackberry patch, calling her daughter's name.

One night she was in the patch near the woods when she heard something crashing through the bushes coming toward her, grunting and panting heavily. She ran to the house as fast as she could and told her husband. He went to the patch, but he only heard the usual night sounds of crickets, frogs, and insects. He thought his wife might have been frightened enough by this experience to discontinue her searches at night, but he was wrong.

The next night, Mrs. Gammon was more determined than ever to look for her child.

"I know she's alive!" she kept saying. "We would have found her body if she were dead!"

"You have to accept that she's gone," Mr. Gammon told his wife. "She's beyond our help now."

"I think someone captured her and is holding her prisoner," said Mrs. Gammon. "We can't give up! Please help me look for her!"

When her husband refused to go, she left home alone and went to the berry patch.

Mr. Gammon knew it was impossible to stop her. He poured himself a cup of coffee and sat at the kitchen table to wait. Several minutes passed. Then he heard Mrs. Gammon's scream cut through the night.

He grabbed his flashlight and raced from the house to her rescue, but she wasn't there! There was nothing in the berry patch. He walked toward the woods, shining his light on the ground. Signs on the ground showed once again that a body had been dragged from the berry patch into the woods. Mr. Gammon called out to his wife, but all he heard was grunting and heavy breathing from something he couldn't see.

He knew it was dangerous to search alone, so he returned quickly to the house and called the sheriff. Again the sheriff brought men with him, and the search began for Mrs. Gammon. The trail led to the edge of the cliff, and that's where they found her. The sight was one they would never be able to put out of their minds for as long as they lived. It would haunt their waking hours and their dreams. They wondered what happened, but Mrs. Gammon could tell them nothing. When they found her, she was clawed to shreds and half eaten.

Residents of the area refused to go into the blackberry patch after that. Dogs kept barking at something unseen in the woods, but they wouldn't enter either. Stories began to circulate that the monster of the blackberry patch was real. Juicy blackberries grew in the patch, but those who were tempted to go near them heard the grunting and heavy breathing, and ran for their lives.

Many people in the neighborhood swore that they saw the ghost of Mrs. Gammon, walking through the blackberry patch at the edge of the woods, looking for her lost daughter. As a ghost, she appeared to be whole.

Because the mystery was never solved, some believe that the horrible unseen thing still stalks the patch for victims. If they get a longing for blackberry cobbler or jam, they head for their favorite market or bakery.

Joy's Incredible Journey

We saved this story for last because it is a tribute to a very dear friend of ours, Joy Pennington. It is hard for us to tell, but because we lived through it ourselves, we know it to be true. Joy died on March 23, 2011, but her dying doesn't mean this is a sad story. She wouldn't have allowed that. Joy's incredible journey to meet death was a beautiful experience for her and all who knew and loved her because she made it so.

Joy and Roberta met in the fall of 1958 when they both entered Berea College. Joy's husband, Lee, entered Berea at the beginning of 1959. Lonnie met Joy and Lee after he and Roberta married in 1977, and they moved across the street from the Penningtons in 1985. The four were all good friends and did many things together, but as with most friendships, their good times were too often taken for granted. After all, there would always be time to do things together!

Joy and Lee were teachers and founders of the Corn Island Storytelling Festival, but they also traveled the world and made documentaries. Joy always seemed blessed with good health, so none of us had any idea anything was wrong until she cracked a bone in her hip. After a while, when the bone didn't heal properly, the doctor ordered X-rays, which showed suspicious spots. The doctor then ordered Joy in for extensive tests.

It was a late October afternoon when Roberta's phone rang. She was surprised to hear Joy's voice because Lee and Joy were supposed to be at the doctor's office getting Joy's test results. Roberta looked at the clock and realized they were probably home by now. That wasn't the case. Actually, they were on their way home.

"Roberta, I need a favor," Joy said.

"Sure," said Roberta. "What do you need?"

There was a tone in Joy's voice that Roberta had not heard before. But she didn't dream of what she was about to hear.

"I have to go on full oxygen," Joy said in that same tone. "They are on their way to our house to set it up now, but Lee and I are stuck in traffic. They may get to the house before we do, so could you watch for them and let them in with your key if they get there first?"

"Absolutely," Roberta said. "But why do you need oxygen?"

"I have stage four cancer," Joy said in a steady voice. "It's in my bones, lungs, brain, sinus cavity—just everywhere."

"Joy, it must be a mistake," said Roberta, not really believing what she had just heard. "You are never sick!"

"It's not a mistake," she said in that same steady voice. "I've seen the X-rays and all the results. They give me two months to live."

Roberta wanted to scream and cry, but she knew what that tone in Joy's voice meant. No crying and no pity. Roberta's heart was crying, though, and she was thinking that Joy's time couldn't possibly be that short. She wanted much more time with her friend.

Joy said that she and Lee were going to discuss how to proceed, but she ultimately decided that she would stay at home and refused chemo and radiation. She agreed to take pain medication, but only enough to make the pain bearable. She wanted to be alert and functioning until the end.

Joy's first rule was that no teary people were allowed to come and visit. That eliminated a lot of friends, because most of them broke down and cried. Of course, she had to limit visitors because she got tired easily, too. Hospice (or Hosparus, as it is now called in Louisville) came to provide care to Joy and to help Lee. Lee considered it an honor to be Joy's main caregiver, and he made sure that Joy got everything she wanted. No caregiver ever did a better job than Lee did for Joy!

Lee and Joy had no family in Louisville. Hosparus was a great help, but there were times when their volunteers weren't available and Lee had to run errands. Lonnie and Roberta cleared their calendars and made themselves available any time day or night if Lee needed someone to sit with Joy. It wasn't a noble gesture or sacrifice on their part. They saw it as a second chance to pay all those visits they had meant to have but had put off until another time. Now time was running out.

The first time Lee called, Roberta was happy to go over, but she knew if she wanted time with Joy, she would have to do things Joy's way. As she walked across the street, she kept telling herself that she could not cry! She thought that being with her dying friend would be so sad and heartbreaking that she would have to go home and bawl her eyes out. But Roberta was wrong.

This visit and the ones to follow turned out to be the most uplifting times of Roberta's life. Lonnie felt the same about the times he went to spend time with Joy. Amazingly, these visits felt completely natural. The friends talked and laughed and remembered things they had shared.

Even though she had no need to economize, Joy still clipped coupons and sent Lee to get dinner for themselves and Lonnie and Roberta. She had her hairdresser and her manicurist come to the house and fix her hair and nails, and she sent Lee shopping for makeup.

She looked so healthy that at one point Roberta said, "Joy, you look so good—do you think they could have made a mistake?"

She said, "No, Roberta. It's going to happen."

Joy was never in denial and sometimes wanted to talk about her cancer. These talks, however, were never morbid. Once Joy wondered aloud what the cancer was doing inside of her.

"Can you feel it?" Roberta asked.

"No," said Joy. "I don't feel anything."

She never asked that her life be extended for her own sake. And when her predicted time to die came in December, she felt fine.

Joy said to Roberta, "I hope I can live long enough to show Lee how to do the taxes."

She read, made lists of favorite things and places, and gave Lee cooking lessons. She and Lee watched the documentaries they had made and relived the wonderful moments of their life together. Joy said she'd had a wonderful life, that she had seen most of the world, and that she had no regrets.

As Christmas approached Joy sent out special Christmas cards with a picture of Lee and her taken the year before at Death Valley. People had to smile at her sense of humor. Christmas came and went, and December ended. Her two months were up, but Joy was very much alive!

In January, Joy invited six of her and Lee's closest friends (Ben and Sonia, Tami and Andy, and Roberta and Lonnie) to celebrate their forty-ninth wedding anniversary. By then, Joy was getting tired easily, so she put a possible time limit on the visit. It was a happy occasion, with no shadow of death spoiling the party.

On Valentine's Day, she had the same six people over. She loved planning these get-togethers, and she saw to it that everybody had a great choice of Valentine desserts to eat.

On Lonnie's birthday on February 28, Joy again invited the same six people to a party. Her rules this time were that the men had to wear suits and the women had to wear dresses. Joy wore a party dress and jewelry and looked better than anybody! It was a birthday Lonnie will never forget.

Joy was doing so well that she began to plan a St. Patrick's Day party for March 17. All these celebrations were held with the understanding that the guests would leave if Joy got tired.

Joy had always eaten healthy foods, but she suddenly surprised everybody by beginning to crave fast food, like Quarter Pounders, or sausage, biscuits, gravy, and eggs.

Since Lee couldn't leave Joy alone to go to the fast food restaurants, Lonnie happily became her banker and delivery man. Joy gave Lonnie money to keep so he could go get her whatever she wanted whenever she called. Joy would gobble the food and say, "Lonnie, this stuff won't hurt you, especially if you're dying anyway!"

March brought early flowers. Joy looked out the window and saw the first crocus of spring blooming in her yard. Lee picked it and put it in a vase for her. At first, it turned to the window for sunlight like all flowers do, but Lee turned it back toward Joy and it never turned away again.

Joy's St. Patrick's Day party was not to be. The cancer began to make noticeable changes. She was no longer strong enough to have people come around to visit.

The day of Roberta's last visit to Joy was a little different from the others. As Roberta started to leave, Joy took her hand and smiled.

"I want to thank you for all you have done for me," she said.

"I was happy to do what I could," Roberta told her. "I love you!"

"I love you, too," she said.

"I'll see you later," Roberta said to Joy, but as she left, she knew she had seen her friend for the last time.

Joy died peacefully on March 23, 2011, with just Lee by her side. It was five months later than the two months the doctors had predicted Joy would live from the time the cancer was diagnosed. If Death had been lurking around to see Joy's spirit break, he was sorely disappointed.

The day Joy died had been filled with severe storm warnings. But they were lifted, and at the exact moment of her death, a friend snapped a picture of the sky. It was filled with a bright light like a sunburst! It was as if the heavens had opened to welcome her in.

When the hearse came to take Joy away, Roberta stood in her driveway to say a silent good-bye to her friend. Suddenly, thunder shook the whole street, and lightning, in the most vivid shades of pink, purple, and gold, danced above Lee and Joy's house. The rain came down gently. As the undertakers carried Joy out of the house, the rain stopped and the sky was calm.

Joy's service was exactly as she wanted it to be. She and Lee had made a DVD together celebrating her life. It said what she wanted to say.

Later, when Lee took Joy's ashes to be scattered at sea as she had requested, small-craft warnings were posted along the coast. The captain and first mate of the boat Lee had hired told Lee they couldn't go out very far because of the choppy water. But at the moment Lee scattered Joy's ashes, the sea became calm. It remained calm all the way back to shore.

Several odd things have happened since Joy's passing that make Lee, Roberta, and Lonnie think that Joy may be coming back now and then to visit. Lee has written his own experiences, but there was one that the three of us shared.

On July 4 of the year Joy died, Lee came across the street for a short visit with Roberta and Lonnie. The three of them were sitting in the living room, talking, when all of them heard the kitchen door open and close. They heard footsteps crossing the room. Lonnie went to the kitchen and checked the door, but it was still closed and locked. No one was there. He came back and sat down, but then they all heard the footsteps again.

Together they said, "Come in, Joy!"

It would have been logical for Joy to join them since the four friends often did things together.

Joy's death left those who loved her with an uplifting feeling instead of a feeling of sadness. Death was not something that came to end her life. It was merely a vehicle to take her to the next place in eternity where she was meant to be.

May we all be so lucky when our time comes.

Thank you, Joy, for letting us be close to you in life and death! We miss you, but we will see you again someday.

Conclusion

In our early years, we had no radio, TV, or computers to entertain us. All that has changed now, but the stories we heard and shared over the years are more important than ever. They link us to our past and the people who are now gone. Technology will never replace them in our lives. We hope these stories will stir some memories for you.

We love a good story, so if you have one to share, please send it to us. You can contact us through Roberta's Web site: robertasimpsonbrown.com.

Places to Visit

Ashland Paramount Art Center is located at 1300 Winchester Avenue, Ashland, Kentucky, 41101. You might meet up with the permanent friendly ghost, a former worker named Joe. Call 606-324-3175.

The Brown Hotel (335 West Broadway, 40202—toll free 888-387-0498) and **The Seelbach Hotel** (500 Fourth Street, 40202—call 502-585-3200) are two of Louisville's finest—and most haunted—hotels. The best way to access these for spooky experiences is to contact Mr. Ghost Walker (Robert Parker) and take his *original* Louisville ghost walks. In our opinion, these are the best-researched and best-presented tours of downtown Louisville, and they include several other haunted sites besides the hotels. Call 502-689-5117 or check Mr. Parker's Web site, www.LouisvilleGhostWalks .com.

For tours of Victorian homes in **Old Louisville** (America's largest Victorian neighborhood), contact David Domine at ghostsofoldLouisville.com. You will enjoy this tour immensely and are likely to encounter a ghost! The tour is well researched and well presented, and it covers a part of Louisville that is not visited in other tours.

Bardstown, Kentucky, has many haunted sites, but two of the best known are **Jailer's Inn** (111 West Stephen Foster Avenue, 40004; on the Web at jailersinn.com, or call 502-348-5551) and **Old Talbot Inn** (107 West Stephen Foster, 40002—call 502-348-3494.) We recommend that you take the Patti Starr tour of downtown Bardstown. We found it very informative and entertaining. Contact Patti at 859-576-5517 for tour information.

LaGrange, Kentucky, is a unique place where a real train comes right through the middle of town and where ghosts come out to be sighted. **The Spirits of LaGrange Tour** is conducted by talented tour guides, such as Barbara Edds, in costume and carrying lanterns. You will hear spellbinding accounts of all the ghostly happenings in LaGrange, one of the most haunted places in Kentucky. This tour is very popular, so call for reservations at 502-291-1766.

For spirits you imbibe and for spirits you may encounter from beyond, try Louisville's **Phoenix Hill Tavern**. Drop in at 644 Baxter Avenue, Louisville, Kentucky, 40204. The phone number is 502-589-4957.

Mammoth Cave (near Park City in south central Kentucky) was described by an early guide as a "grand, gloomy, and peculiar place." He could add now that it is also haunted. To book a tour, call 270-758-2181.

Acknowledgments

We thank our friend, Dewayne VanderEspt, who always comes to our rescue, especially when we are baffled by computers.

We thank our neighbor, Salvador Doggie, for visiting us and staying nearby to give his unconditional support while we are writing. His sweet little spirit is always a delight and an inspiration. (Thanks, Jill Baker and Lee Pennington, for sharing him.)

A special thanks to Lee Pennington for his guidance and support through the years. Without him, we would probably never have written our books.

We are especially grateful to our manuscript editor, Donna Bouvier; to Ashley Runyon, acquisitions editor; and to all the staff at the University Press of Kentucky, who helped us so much with this book.

About the Authors

Roberta Simpson Brown and **Lonnie E. Brown** were both born in Russell Springs, Kentucky. Roberta had one sister, and Lonnie had three sisters and two younger brothers. Their families, along with other relatives and neighbors, got together often and joined in the Kentucky tradition of storytelling.

Lonnie first shared stories with the people close to him, who responded with sidesplitting laughter and encouraged him to write the tales he told and experienced. The result was his first book, *Stories You Won't Believe*. He later coauthored *Spooky, Kooky Poems for Kids* and *Spookiest Stories Ever: Four Seasons of Kentucky Ghosts* with his wife, Roberta. An accomplished musician and golfer, Lonnie enjoys nature, reading, and doing paranormal investigations with Roberta and their friends.

Roberta also told stories, but she preferred to write. She used storytelling in her classroom as a teacher, but she never thought about being a professional storyteller until her friends, Lee and Joy Pennington, got her involved in the Corn Island Storytelling Festival, which they founded. Her first book, *The Walking Trees and Other Scary Stories*, resulted from her work with the festival. She is also the author of seven other books and has recorded three CDs of her original stories. Roberta has appeared on programs at festivals, workshops, schools, libraries, and conferences from coast to coast. She has been on National Public Radio, the Voice of America, and the Lifetime television show *Beyond Chance*.

Married since 1977, Lonnie and Roberta live in Louisville and continue to write and enjoy ghost tales, as well as actual ghosts. They like to hear from readers. Please visit Roberta's Web site, robertasimpsonbrown.com.